Year 1
Workbook

Pearson

Published by Pearson Education Limited, 80 Strand, London, WC2R 0RL.
www.pearson.com/international-schools

Copies of official specifications for all Pearson Edexcel qualifications may be found on the website:
https://qualifications.pearson.com

Text © Pearson Education Limited 2023
Produced by Just Content Ltd
Designed by PDQ Media Digital Media Solutions
Typeset by PDQ Media Digital Media Solutions
Picture research by Straive Ltd
Original illustrations © Pearson Education Limited 2023
Cover design © Pearson Education Limited 2023

The right of Lesley Butcher to be identified as the author of this work has been asserted by her in accordance with the
Copyright, Designs and Patents Act 1988.

First published 2023

26
12

British Library Cataloguing in Publication Data
A catalogue record for this book is available from the British Library

ISBN 978 1 292 43328 8

Printed in Italy by L.e.g.o. S.p.A.

Contents

Living things

The world is full of living things. Humans, plants and animals are all living things. Some things, like sticks, were once alive. Some things, like rocks, are non-living.

In this topic we will learn:

- that animals are living things
- that plants are living things
- the differences between living and non-living things
- how animals change as they grow
- how plants change as they grow.

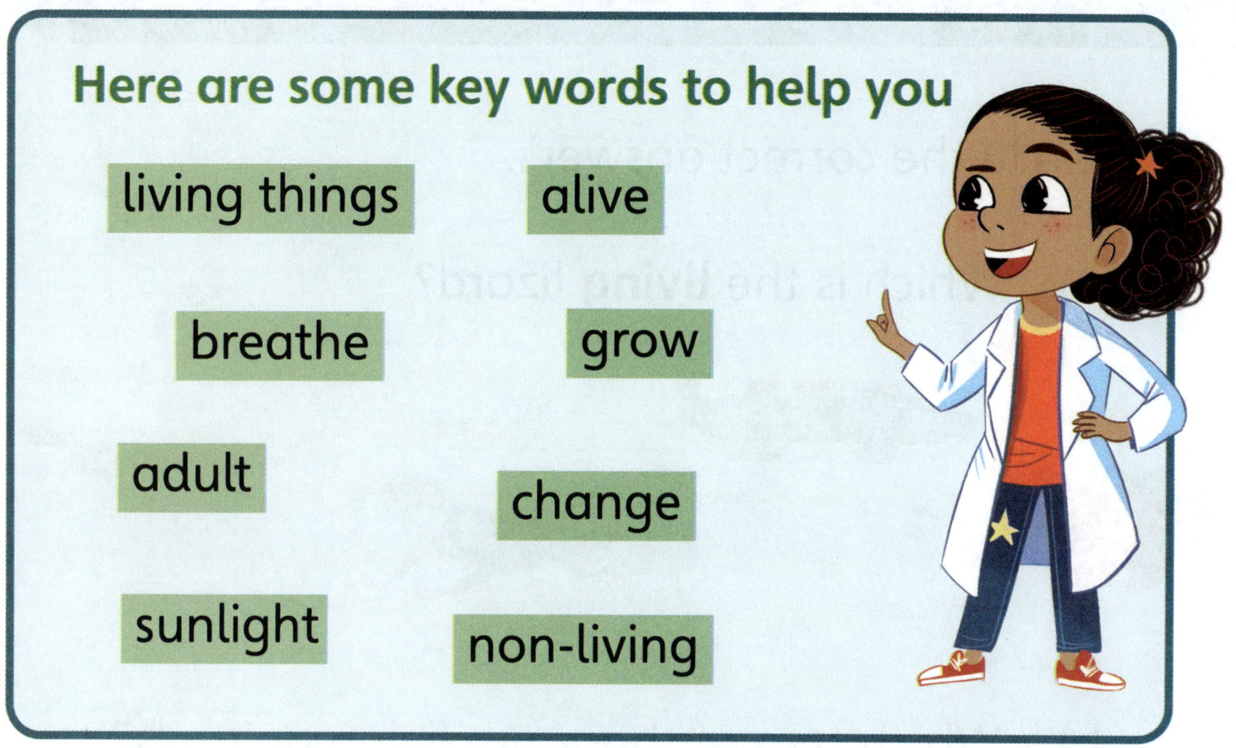

Choose two key words from the box above.
Write or draw what they mean.

Animals are living things

1 Circle the correct answers.

a) Which is the **living** lizard?

b) Which **two** of these are living animals?

c) Which picture shows **two living things**?

2 The pictures show three different animals.

What are all the animals doing that shows they are alive?

____

3 a) This toy is **not** a living thing.
        The girl blows on the toy.
        What can the toy do now?
        Circle the correct answer.

breathe   eat   grow   sense   move

   b) Write a list of things that the girl can do.

____

____

Plants are living things

1. Circle the living tree.

2. Circle the living things in the picture.

3. Circle **one** thing plants need to make their food.

dish   light   meat   shop

4 a) What is this plant doing? Circle the correct answer.

growing

singing

talking

walking

b) Draw what you think the plant will look like next.

5 Write **four** things that living plants can do.

I. _________________   2. _________________

3. _________________   4. _________________

Living or non-living?

1. Count how many beetles are alive. ☐

2. Circle the living tiger.

3. a) Complete the label with the name of the equipment.

b) Why is this flower in water?

____

4 Draw a line from each picture to show if the object is **dead** or **non-living**.

dead

non-living

Are robots alive?

1 What is this robot doing?
Circle the correct answer.

breathing   eating   growing   moving

2 

Write the name of **one** living thing in the picture.

____

3 Write the word **robot** or **living** under
each picture.

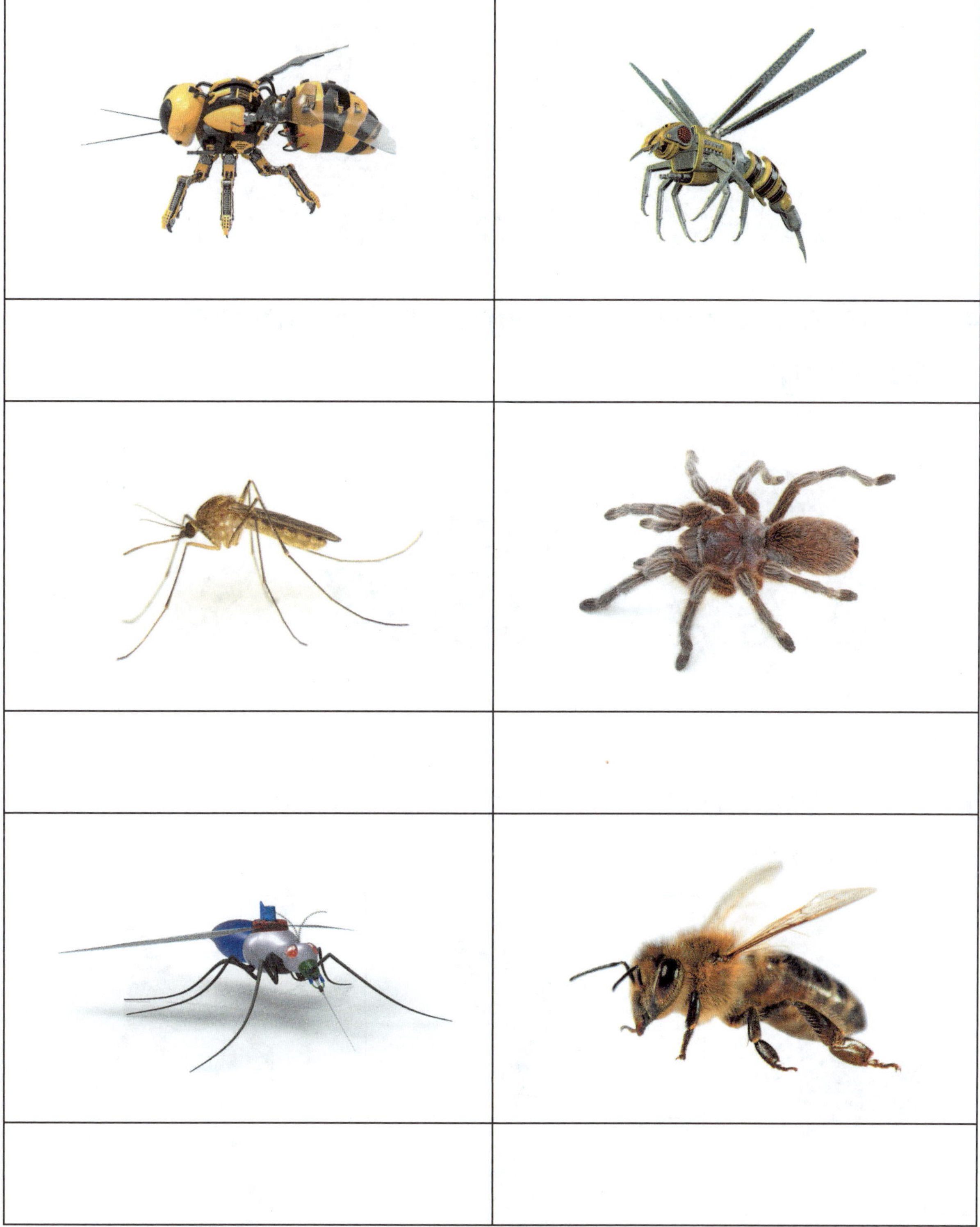

Animals grow and change

1. Circle the **oldest** bird.

2. Circle the picture showing the **youngest** ducklings.

3. Circle the adult that the baby animal grows into.

baby animal

4 Circle the adult gorilla.

5 Draw the baby for each of these animals.

Baby		
Adult		

Watching plants grow and change

1. The picture shows a bean growing.

   a) Label the bean seed.

   b) Label the soil.

2. Joel plants some seeds in pots of soil.

   Write **three other** things the seeds need to grow into big plants.

1. _______________________

2. _______________________

3. _______________________

3   This bean has split open.

    a)   What is happening to
        the bean?

       ____

    b)   Circle the new bean plant.

    c)   Where is the new plant's food store?

       ____

4   The pictures show a seed growing into a plant.

    Draw what you think the plant will look like in
    pot 3.

What have I learned?

1 I can tell the difference between living and non-living things.

I know this because non-living things **cannot**

____

____

2 I know that plants are living things.

I know this because plants can _______________

____

I can draw a picture of some plants.

3 I know that animals are living things.

I know this because animals can ___________

____

I can draw a picture of some animals.

4 I understand that animals change as they grow.

I know this because baby animals like kittens

change into ___________________

5 I understand that plants change as they grow.

I know this because seeds change into ________

____

Myself

Humans are living things. We all look different, but we have many things that are the same. We grow and change as we get older.

In this topic we will learn:

- that humans need three important things to stay alive
- that humans have five senses and five sense organs
- how to identify the outside parts of a human body
- about things that are similar and different between humans
- that humans grow and change as they grow older.

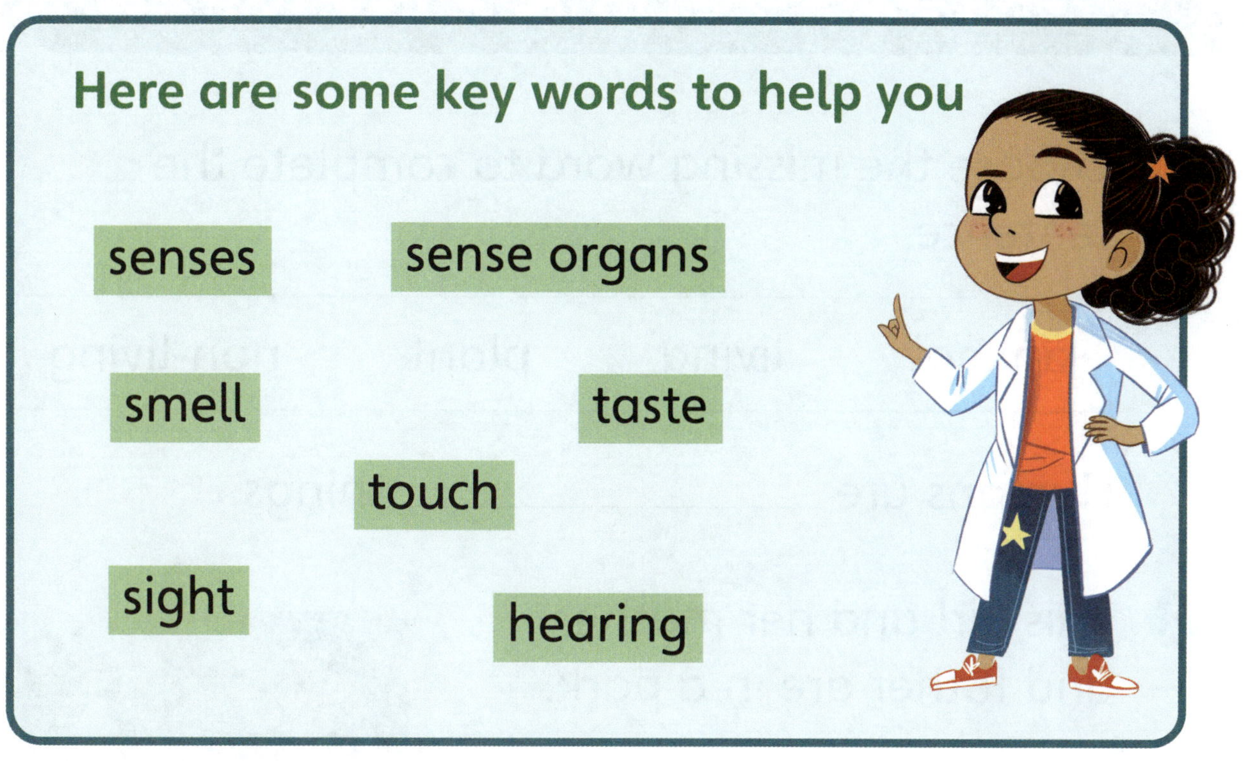

Choose two key words from the box above.
Write or draw what they mean.

Humans are living things

1. Choose the missing word to complete the sentence.

animal	living	plant	non-living

Humans are _________________ things.

2. This girl and her mother and father are in a park.

Put **one** tick (✓) **in each row** to show which things in the picture are **living** and which are **non-living**.

	Living	Non-living
grass		
girl		
scarf		
trees		
mother		
shirt		
father		

3. What do human babies drink to stay alive?

____

4 Put **one** tick (✓) **in each row** of the table to show whether it is an **adult** or a **child**.

Picture	Adult?	Child?

Staying alive

1 Circle the **drink** in this picture.

2 Choose **three** words to complete the sentence.

air   cars   food   houses   light   soil   water

To stay alive, humans need _________________

and _________________ and _________________.

3 What is this girl doing to help her stay alive?

____

4 Circle the food that contains the most water.

5 Choose the correct words to complete the sentences about the picture. Use each word once.

alive	breathing	water	in	out

This human is _________________ out air.

She breathes air _________________ and out to stay _________________.

The air she breathes _________________ has _________________ from her body in it.

Five senses

I   a)   Draw lines to match each sense organ with the change it detects.

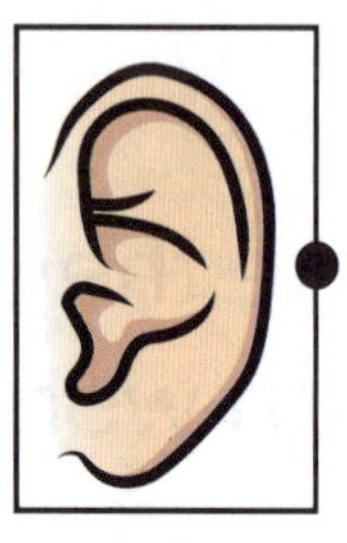

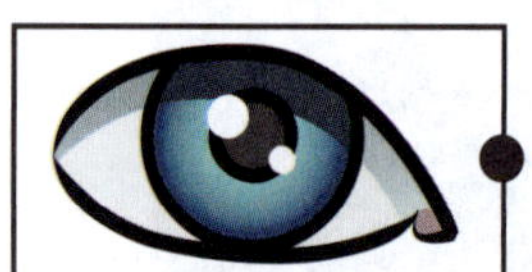

smell of food

sound of animals

light from a lamp

b)   Name **two** more sense organs not shown in the pictures above.

1. _______________________________________

2. _______________________________________

2 Write the name of the sense organ under each picture.

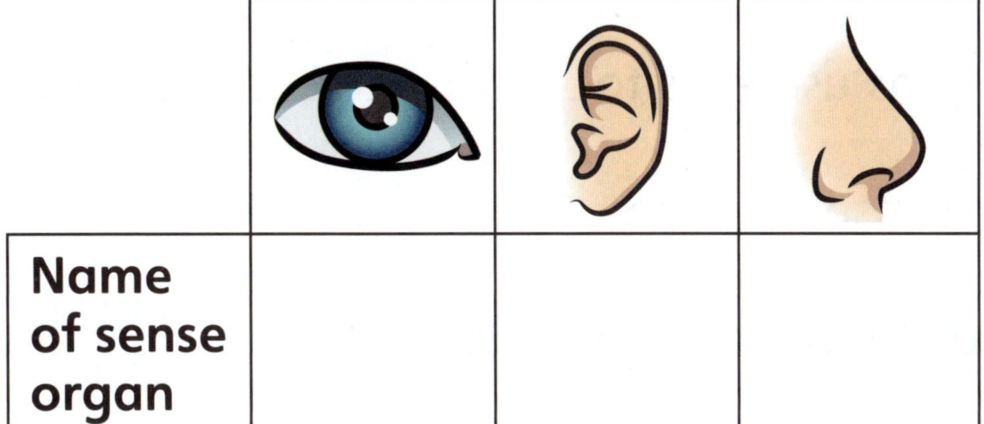

Name of sense organ			

3 Write the name of **one** sense organ in each space.

We use this sense organ for hearing.

____

We use this sense organ for seeing.

____

We use this sense organ to feel things.

____

We use this sense organ for smelling.

____

Seeing things

1. Complete the sentences about eyes.

   Humans use eyes to _________________ things.

   This sense is called _________________.

2. What changes do eyes detect?

   Tick (✓) the correct rows.

Change	Do eyes detect this?
light and dark	
hot and cold	
things moving	
sounds	
colours	
smells	

3. Make a tally chart of eye colours in your class. Write in the colours you need.

Eye colour	Tally	Total

4. Work with a partner.

Cover one of your eyes with your hand.

Keep BOTH eyes OPEN.

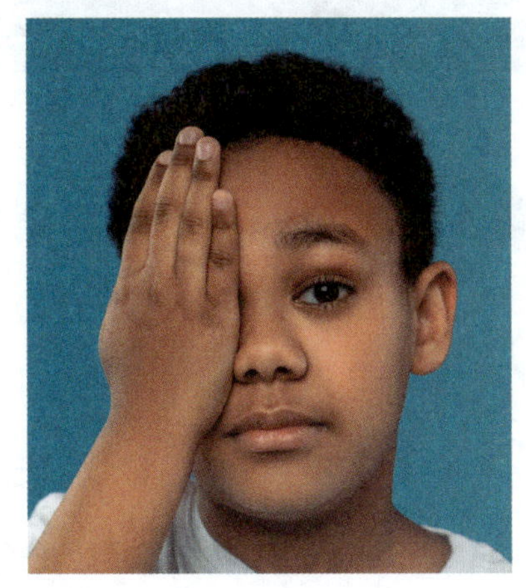

Tell your partner to look carefully at the **pupil** of your **uncovered** eye.

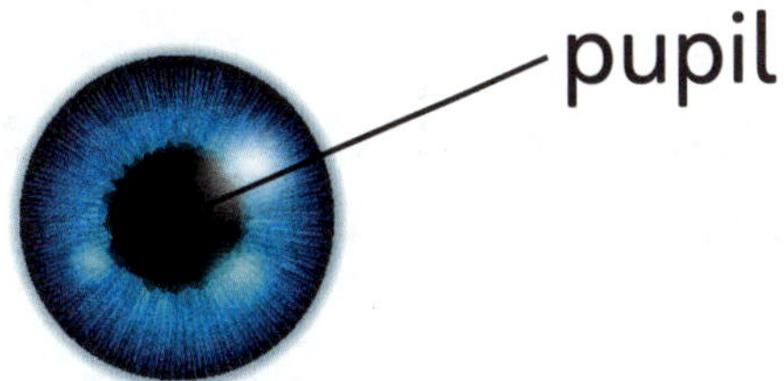

Take your hand away. Does the pupil they are watching change size?

Now watch your partner do this.

Draw what you see.

Eye with big pupil	**Eye with small pupil**

Smell

1 a) Circle the sense organ we use to smell things.

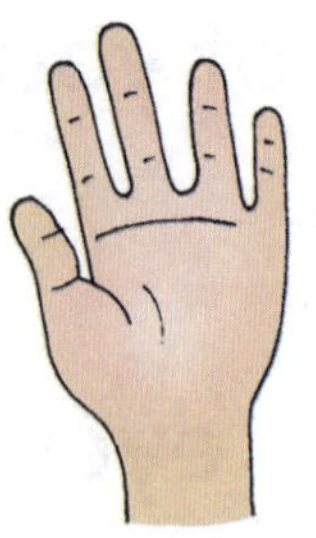
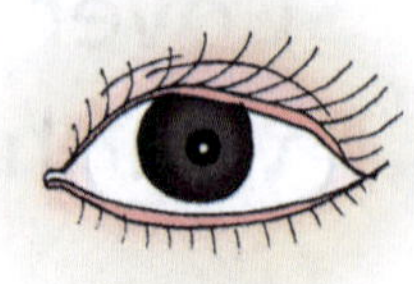

b) Name the sense organ you circled.

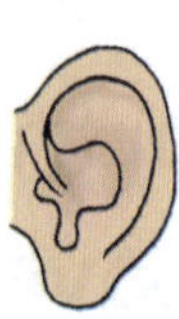
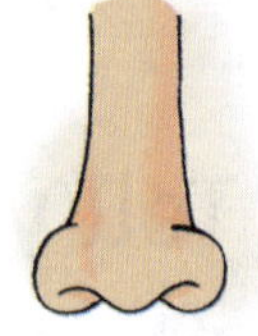

____

2 Put **one** tick (✓) **in each row** of the table to show if you **like** or **do not like** the smell.

Picture	I like this smell	I do not like this smell
flowers		
dirty socks		
spices		
fresh fish		

3 a) Make a tally chart to show which smells 20 people in your class like. Include yourself!

Smells we like	Tally	Total

b) Class One drew a bar chart of their results.

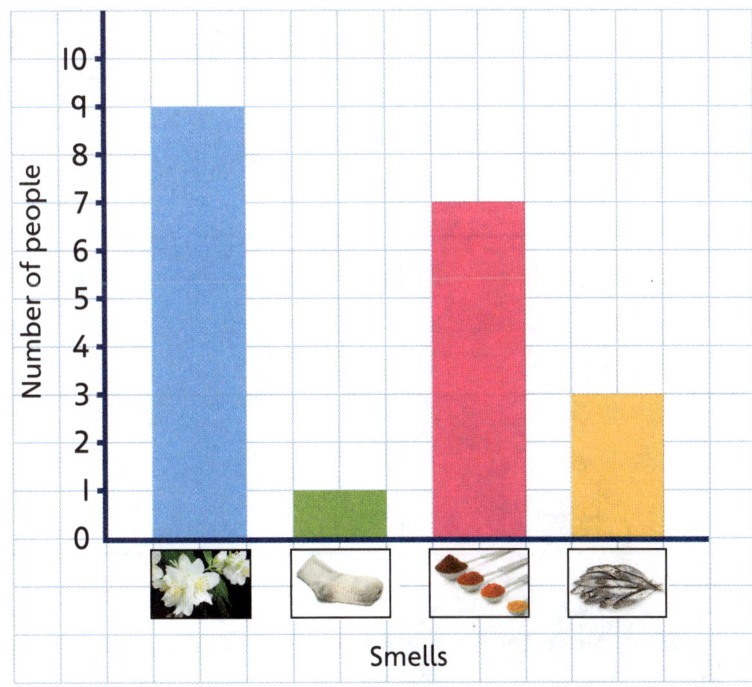

Which smell do most people in Class One like?

____

Taste

1. a) Circle the sense organ used to taste food.

     ear   eye   skin   tongue

   b) Which other sense organ helps us to taste by smelling food? _______________

2. We sense different groups of tastes.

   Put **one** tick (✓) **in each row** of the table to show if you **like** or **do not like the taste.**

Taste group	Picture	I like this taste	I do not like this taste
sweet			
sour			
umami			
salty			
bitter			

3 Write **three** of your favourite foods.
Which taste group are they in?

	Foods I like to eat	Taste group
1		
2		
3		

4 Choose words from the box to complete the sentences.

Use a different word in each space.
You will not need to use all the words.

red   nice   bad   sour   better   protect   ill

Food that is going ________________ does not taste very nice.

Milk tastes ________________ when it is very old.

Our sense of taste helps to ________________ us from eating something that might make us ________________.

Hearing

1 Sit quietly and listen for sounds. Tick (✓) the sounds you can hear. There are four spaces for you to write in and tick other sounds.

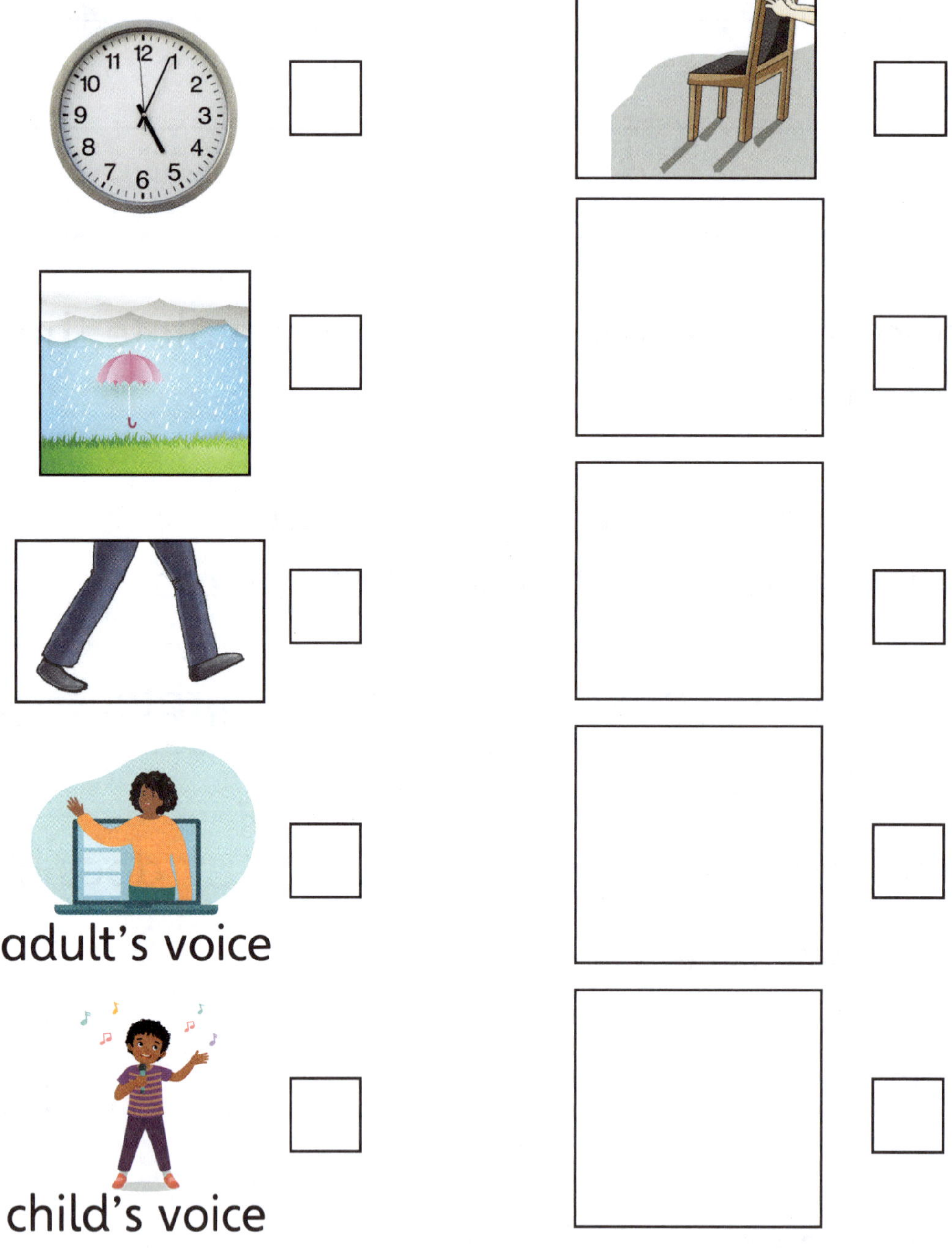

2 Which sense organ do humans use to hear sounds? _______________________

3 We can hear animals make sounds.

Draw lines to match each animal to another animal that makes similar sounds.

Touch

1. a) Which sense do we use to feel things?

   ____

   b) Which sense organ do we use to feel things?

   ____

2. a) Circle a word to show who might read this book.

   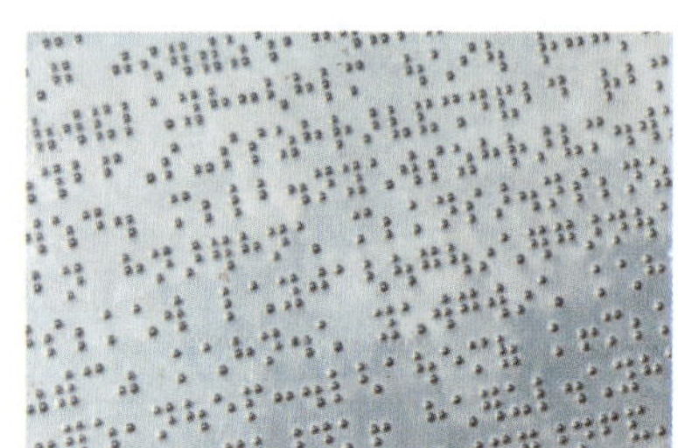

   Someone who **cannot**

   hear   listen   see   touch

   b) This is a braille alphabet.

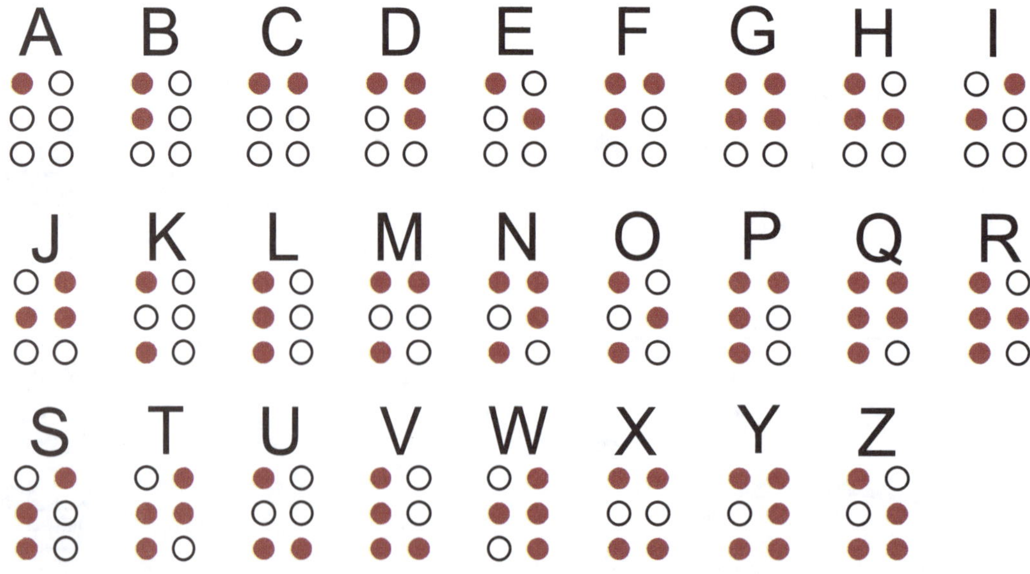

Write your first (given) name using braille.
Put **one** letter or set of dots in each box.

Write your name in letters on this row.										
Draw braille dots on this row.										

3 Draw your hand.

Use a line and the words below to label your drawing.

finger   thumb

Body parts

1 The diagram shows a human.

a) Draw a label line and write the word to label each of these parts.

arm   ear   leg   neck   head   finger

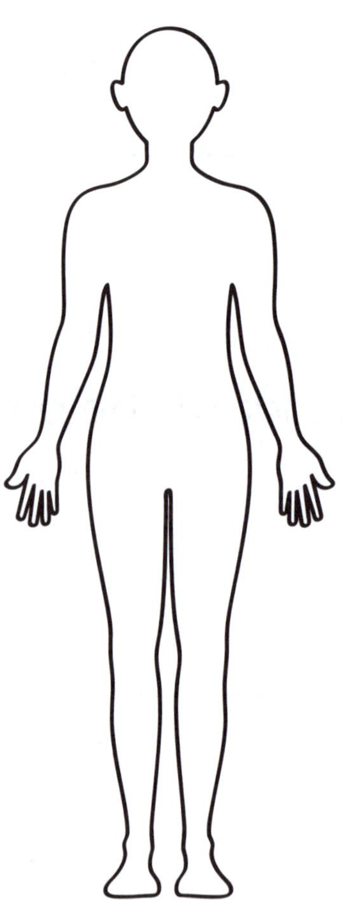

b) Draw these things on the diagram above.

eyes   mouth   nose   toes

c) Draw a circle round a **knee** and a **wrist**.

2 The scale shows 10 centimetres (cm).

a) Put the bottom of your middle finger at 0 and mark the length of your finger on the scale with an arrow (↑).

b) Is your **thumb longer** or **shorter** than your middle finger? _______________

c) Do you have any **fingers** that are **longer** than your middle finger?

    If so, how many? _______________

3 The names of some body parts are jumbled here. Find five hidden body parts.

s	h	c	b	e
l	e	g	p	y
h	a	n	d	e
z	d	a	r	m

1 The picture shows a family.
Use the numbers to answer the questions.

| 1 | 2 | 3 | 4 |

a) Which people have **short** hair?

____

b) Which people have **dark** hair?

____

c) Which people are **children**?

____

2 Some human thumbs bend more than others.

This thumb bends a lot. Does yours?

Draw the shape of your thumb in this box.

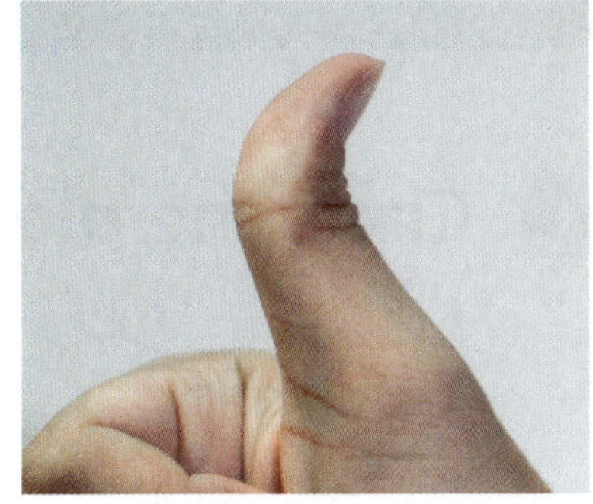

3 Clasp your hands like this.

Now cross one thumb over the other.

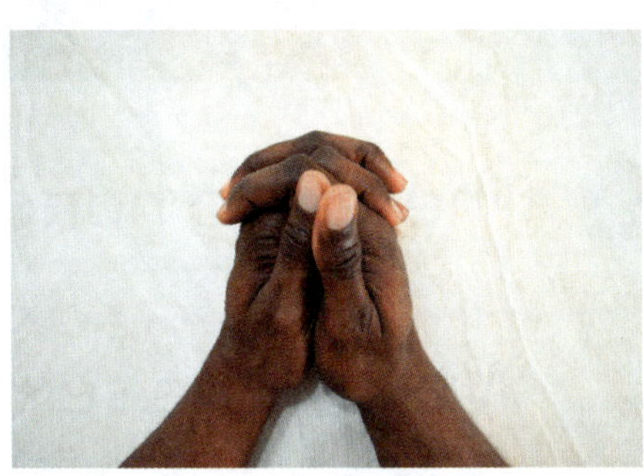

a) Which thumb feels better on top, your right or your left thumb? _______________

b) Can you find someone who differs? Who?

____

Humans grow and change

1 Circle the **oldest** person.

2 These two hands look different.

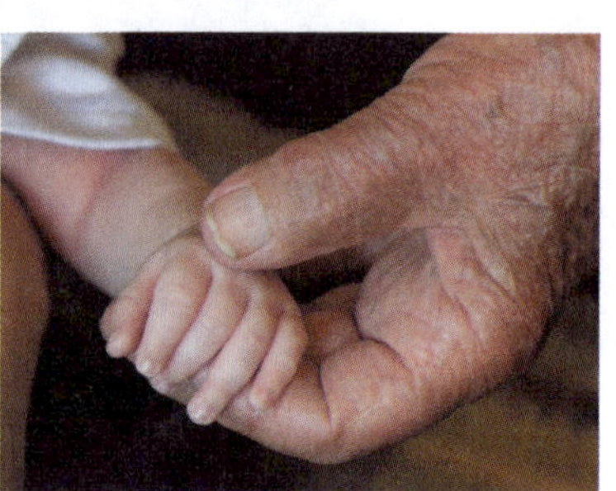

Write some sentences of your own about the differences between the two hands.

____

____

____

____

3 a) Draw a picture of yourself now.

b) **Imagine** what you will look like when you are an adult. Draw a picture.

What have I learned?

1 I know that humans need three important things to stay alive.

I know this because I can list the three things as

_________________ and _________________ and

_________________.

2 I know that humans have five senses and five sense organs. I know that humans use sense organs to detect changes in their surroundings.

I know this because I can list five senses and write the sense organ that is used.

sense	sense organ used
_________________	_________________
_________________	_________________
_________________	_________________
_________________	_________________

3 I can identify the outside parts of a human body.

I know this because I can name six outside parts of a human body.

__________   __________   __________

__________   __________   __________

4 I can compare things that are similar and different between humans.

I know this because I can see two people in my class with similar __________________.

I can also see two people in my class with different __________________.

5 I understand that humans grow and change as they grow older.

I know this because when I was a baby I could **not** __________________.

Animals

Scientists group living things. Animals are one big group. Some animals have backbones. Some animals also have fur or feathers. Let us see what some of them look like.

In this topic we will learn:

- how to observe and describe some animal features
- how to group vertebrates into five groups
- about how animals move
- how animals grow and change as they grow older
- about the different types of food animals eat.

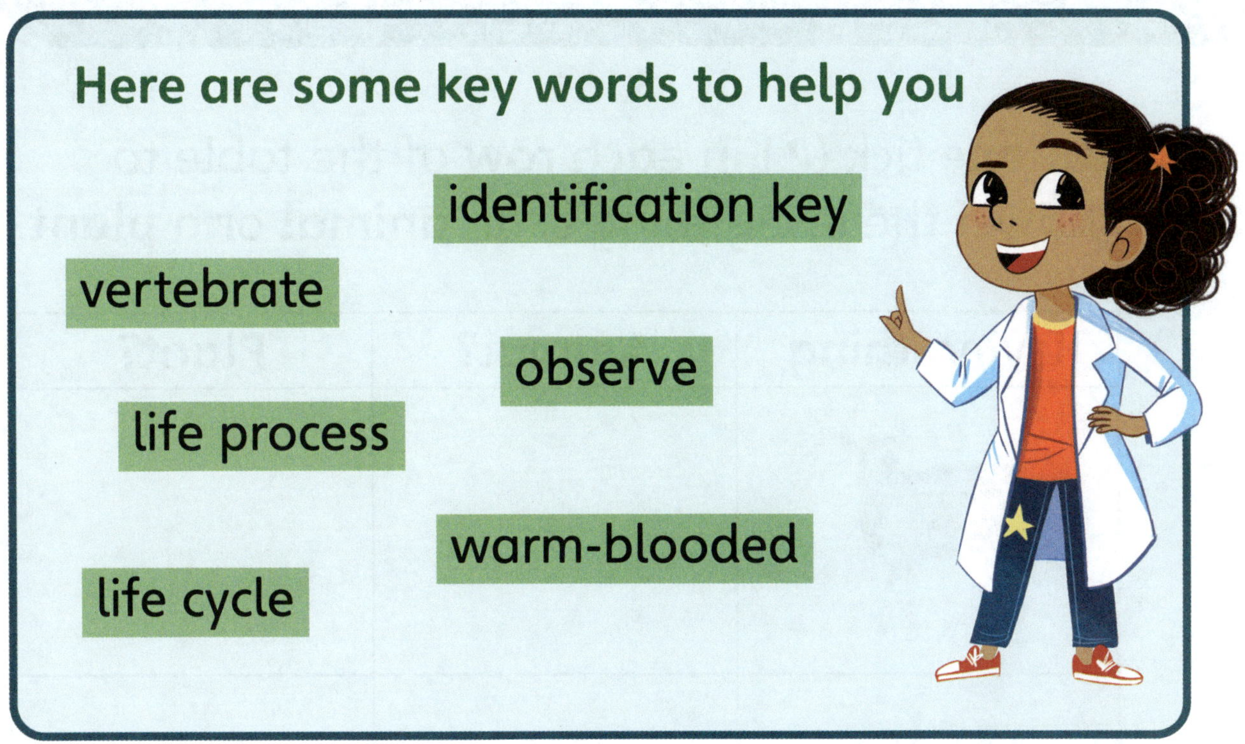

Choose two key words from the box above.
Write or draw what they mean.

1. Put **one** tick (✓) **in each row** of the table to show if the living thing is an **animal** or a **plant.**

Living thing	Animal?	Plant?

2

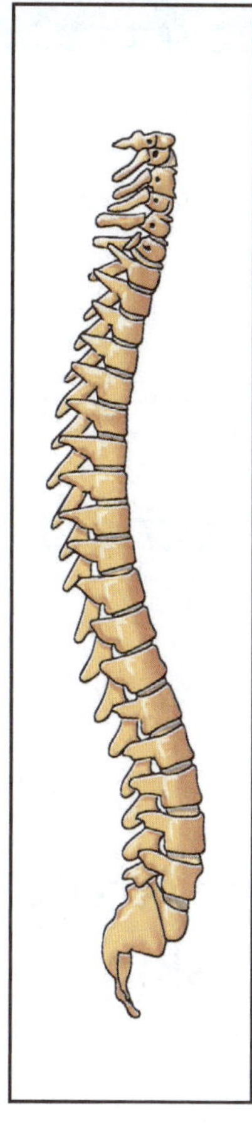

a) Where in your body can you find bones like this?

____

b) Draw a circle on the diagram to show where your head is.

c) What is another name for this long group of bones?

Circle your answer.

spike   spine   spade   spindle

d) What are the small bones in the picture called?

____

3 This animal is a vertebrate.

Draw a line and write a word to label the part that shows it is a vertebrate.

Vertebrate groups

1 Draw lines to match each animal with a feature of the animal.

feathers

dry, scaly skin

fur

thin, moist skin

fins to swim

2 This animal has a backbone.

a) Draw a label line and write a word to show its backbone.

b) What are all animals with backbones called?

____

3 Sully and Victor are in different animal groups.

Write the name of their group under each picture.

______________________   ______________________

What is a key?

1 Use the key to write letter A, B, C or D under each animal picture.

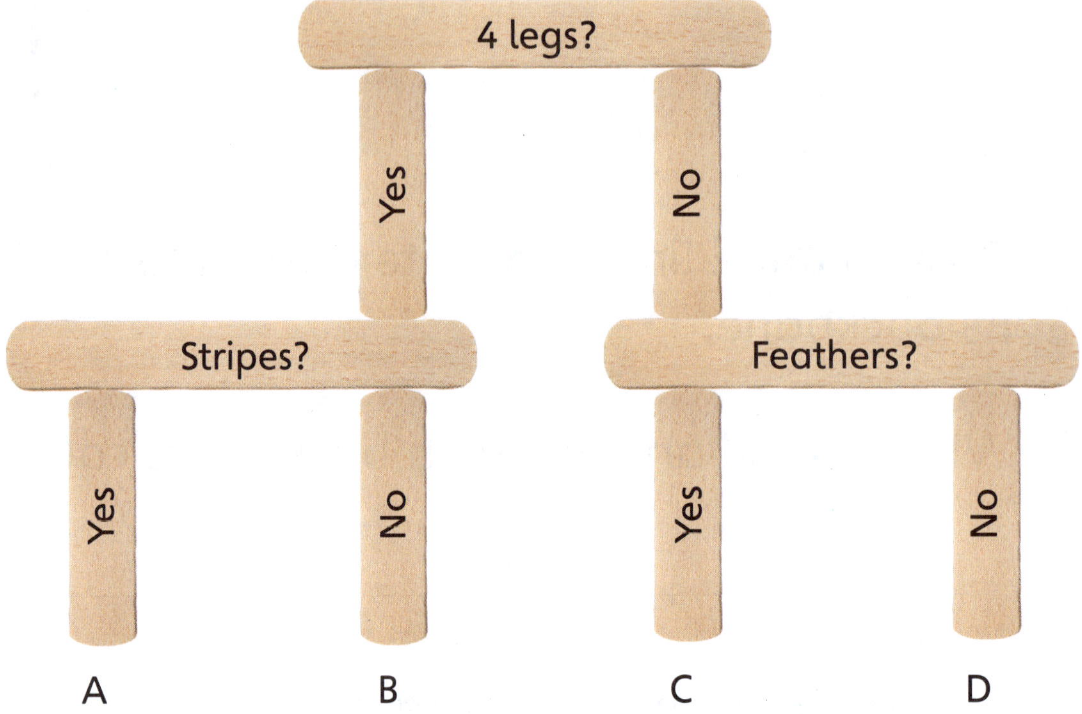

2 Use the key to write letter P, Q, R or S under each animal picture.

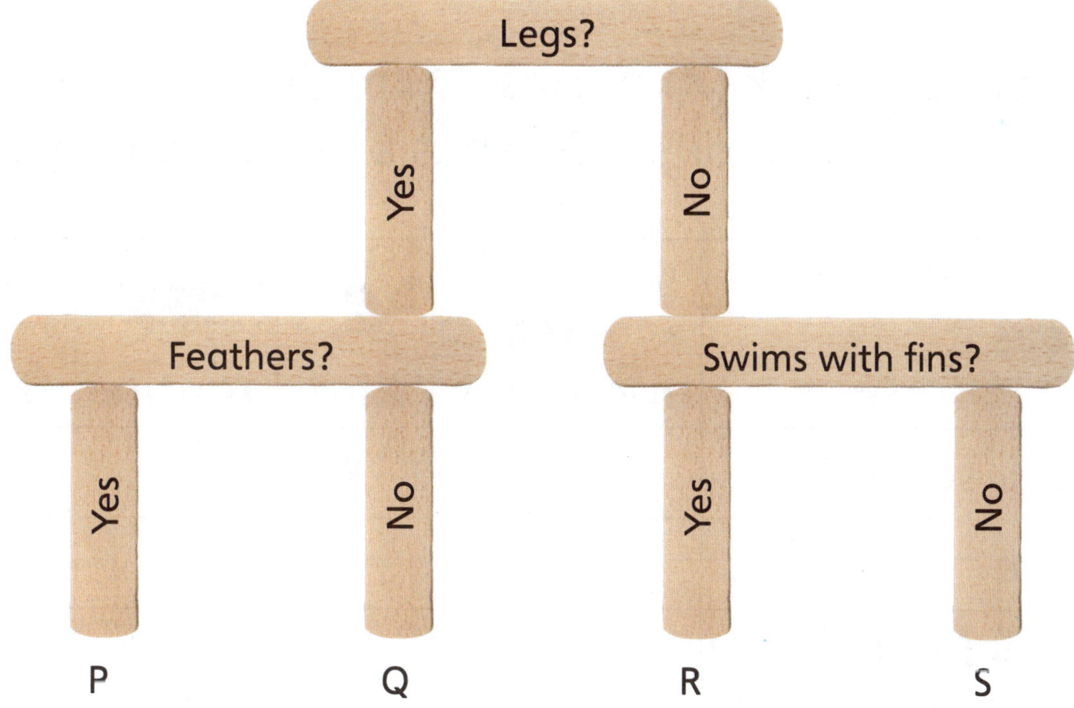

Differences between vertebrate groups

1 a) Put a tick (✓) or cross (✗) to describe the animal groups. One has been done for you.

Does it…	mammal	bird	reptile	fish
have scales?	✗	✗	✓	✓
have fur or hair?				
have feathers?				
swim with fins?				

b) Find the row with **more than one tick (✓)**.

Write that question in the top box of the key opposite.

c) Now find the row with a **tick for fish** but **not reptiles**.

Write that question after the **first yes** on the key.

Write **fish** or **reptile** as the answer in the two blank answer boxes.

d) Pick a third question for the empty box on the key.

Write **mammal** or **bird** as the answer in the two blank answer boxes.

Well done! You have made your own key!

Life processes

1 Write the name of the life process shown in each picture.

____

____

____

____

2 Which of these is **not** a life process?
Circle your answer.

growth   movement   nutrition   washing

3 Complete the table about three life processes.

Life process	Description
	increasing in size
nutrition	
	going to another place or changing position

4 Put **one** tick (✓) in each row to show which life process is described.

	Movement	Growth	Nutrition
a bird eating a worm			
becoming taller			
having noodles for lunch			
a cheetah running			

Animals move in different ways

1 Draw lines to match each animal to the way it is moving.

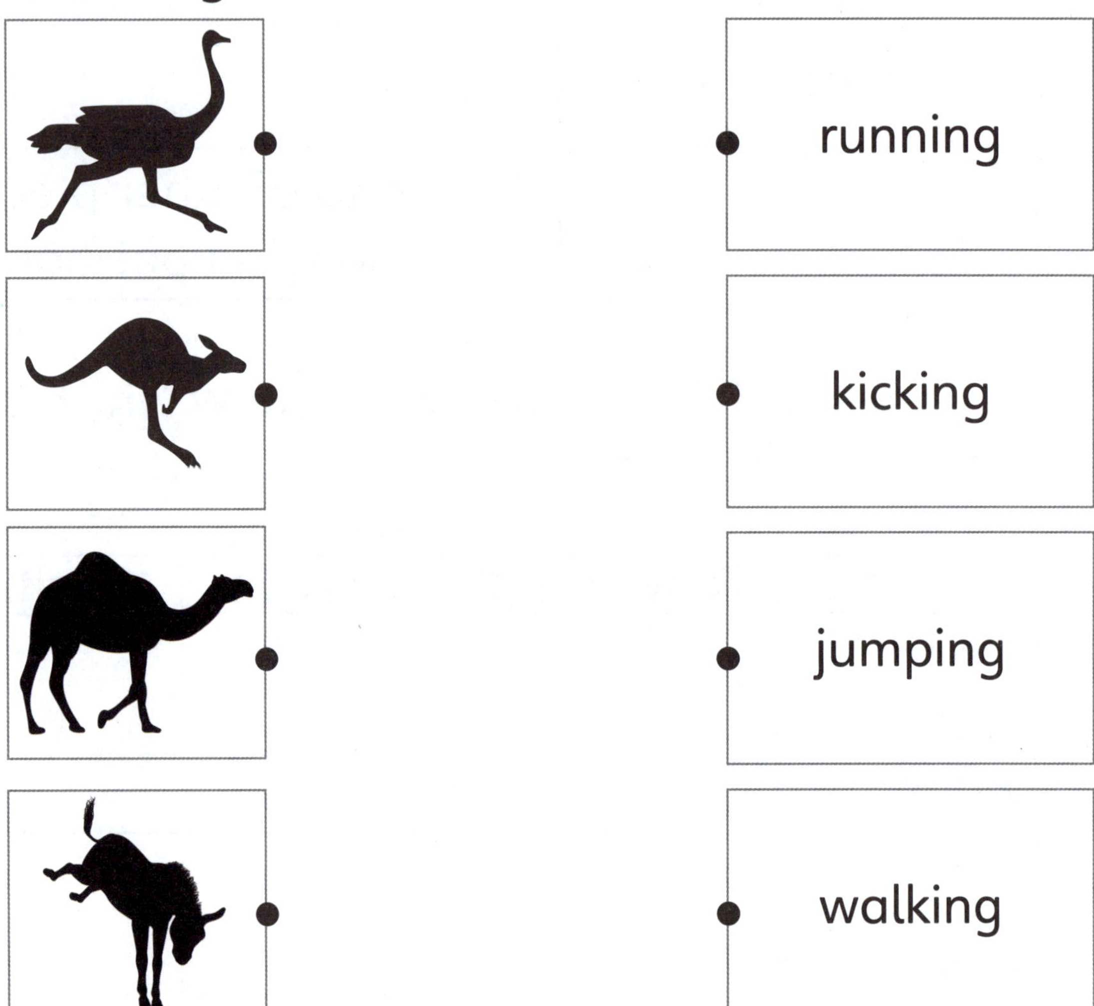

2 a) Circle the animal below that is moving.

b) What are the other animals doing?

____

3 a) Draw an animal that is climbing.

b) Draw an animal that is swimming.

4 Write some ways in which birds move.

____

____

Animals grow

1 Circle the baby birds.

2 Draw lines to match each baby animal to the adult it grows into.

3 This is a kitten.

a) What do we call an adult kitten?

____

b) What is the kitten drinking?

____

c) Draw what you think this kitten will look like as an adult.

4 Write **two** ways that the adult penguins differ from the baby penguins.

1. _______________________________

2. _______________________________

Big eggs and small eggs

1 a) What do we call this place where birds lay their eggs?

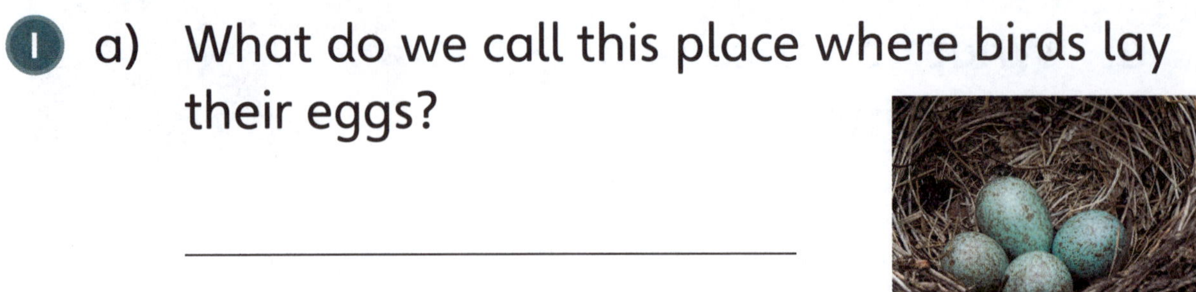

____

b) What is growing inside the eggs?

____

c) Describe the eggs in the picture.

____

____

____

d) Circle **one** egg that is similar to the ones above.

e) What is the number of the largest egg? ☐

2 Write one word from the box in each space.

measuring   different   compare   observations

Scientists look at things to make ________________.

Scientists find out how tall things are by ________________ them.

Scientists ________________ things by looking at how similar they are and how they are ________________.

3 Write one way eggs A and B are similar and one way they differ.

A  B 

Similar ____

Different ____

Birds grow and change

1 Circle **two** words to show where birds lay eggs.

water   nest   land   house   bed

2 All these pictures show ducks.

a)   Which letters show **living** ducks? ___, ___, ___

b)   Which letter shows **adult** ducks? ___

c)   Which group of living ducks is the **oldest**? ___

3 a)   Write 1, 2, 3 or 4 under each picture to show the order in which they happen.

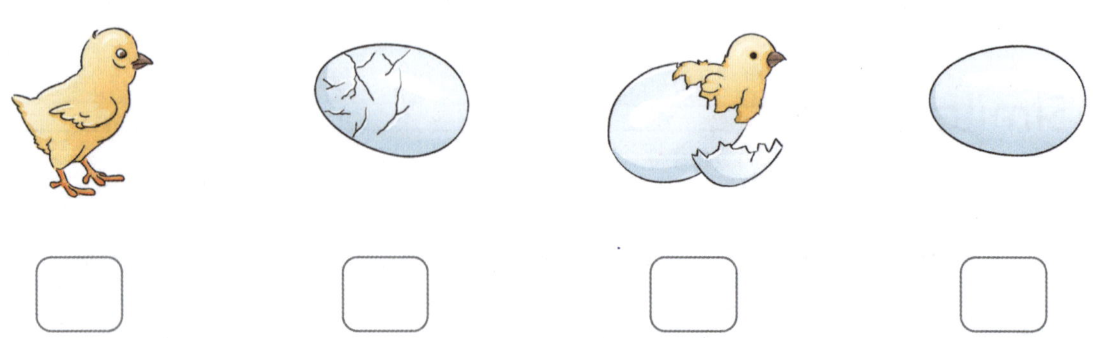

b)   What is the outside of an egg called?

____

c)   What does the chick use to crack the egg

open? _______________________________

4 a)   Label **head**, **foot**, **neck** and **beak** on
this duck.

Use a line and a word each time.

b)   What colour feathers can you see on
this duck?

____

____

____

Reptiles

1 This is the head end of a crocodile.

a) Label its **scales**, **eyes**, **mouth** and **teeth**
     with a line and a word each time.

b) Circle the crocodile's **leg**.

c) Name a reptile that does **not** have legs.

____

d) Crocodiles have a backbone. This means

     they are ________________________________.

e) Describe the crocodile's skin.

____

____

2 a) The diagram shows the life of a turtle.

Complete the title of the diagram.

Life c___________ of a t___________

b) Write one of these by each picture.

eggs   adult   egg hatching   baby turtle

c) Turtles belong to which of these groups? Circle your answer.

mammals   birds   amphibians   reptiles

d) Where does a turtle lay her eggs?

____

Amphibians

1. The diagram shows how a frog changes.

a) Write a title for the diagram.

Title: _______________________________

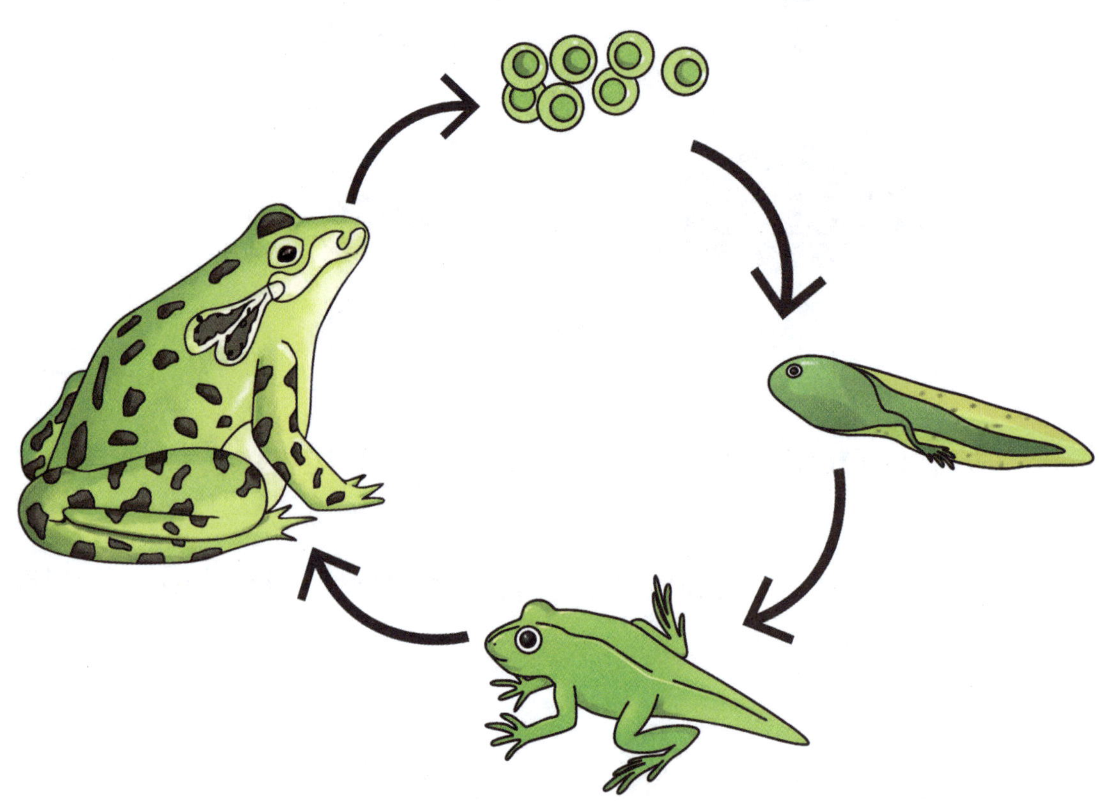

b) Label these things on the diagram.

eggs   adult   baby frog   tadpole

c)   How many legs does an adult frog have?

____

d)   What do frogs cover their eggs in?

____

2 Circle **one** word each time.

a)   How do tadpoles move in water?

run   jump   walk   swim

b)   How do adult frogs move on land?

jump   run   fly   skip

3 Frogs have a backbone and thin, moist skin.

Write **two** groups this puts them in.

___________________ and ___________________

4 Write **three** life processes that frogs can do.

1. ___________________   2. ___________________

3. ___________________

Nutrition

1 a) What is this animal doing?

____

b) Which life process is this?

____

2 Write **four** things that animals need to eat food to be able to do.

1. ____________________________

2. ____________________________

3. ____________________________

4. ____________________________

3 a) What does *warm-blooded* mean?

____

b) Circle **two** groups of vertebrates that are warm-blooded.

mammals   fish   reptiles   birds   amphibians

4 Find out what some animals you know like to eat. Draw and name the animals too.

Animal name and picture	Food it likes

Eating and moving

1 a) What do these animals eat?

Giant panda _______________________

Koala _______________________

Hummingbird _______________________

b) Which life process is eating?

____

2 a) Complete the table for these three animals.

Animal	Which animal group is it in?	Is it warm blooded?
giant panda		
koala		
hummingbird		

b) Which of the three animals can fly?

____

c) Which life process is flying?

____

3 a) Think of an animal you like.

   Draw it with its food and label what it
   is eating.

   b) Draw one animal that moves fast and one
   animal that moves very slowly.

   Label your pictures.

Different diets

1 a) Circle the life process shown in the picture.

nutrition   growth

walking

b) What sort of food do giraffes eat?

____

2 The zebra is running away from the lion.

zebra

a) Which life process is running? ________________

b) Suggest why the zebra is running away.

____

____

c) Predict what will happen if the lion catches the zebra. ________________

____

3 a) What plants do you eat in your diet? Name some.

____

____

b) Draw **two** *different* meals that you like to eat.

Draw label lines and write words to show what is on each plate.

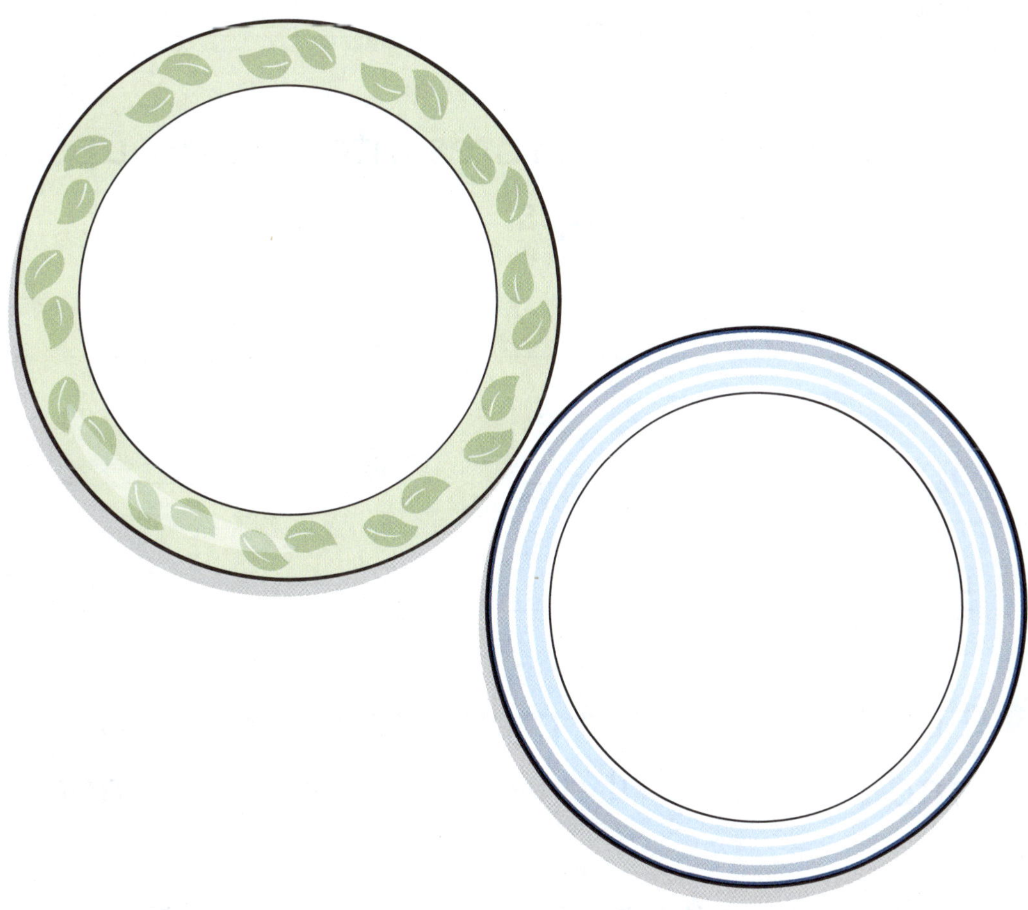

What have I learned?

1. I can observe and describe animal features.

   I can list three parts of a crocodile.

   1. _________________   2. _________________

   3. _________________

2. I know that some animals are vertebrates because they have a _____________ made of little bones called _____________.

3. I can group vertebrates into five groups.
   I can list the groups.

   1. _________________   2. _________________

   3. _________________   4. _________________

   5. _________________

4. I understand that movement is a life process, and I can describe ways in which animals move.

   I can name two ways in which animals move.

   _________________   _________________

5 a) I understand that growth is a life process, and that all animals grow and change as they become older.

I can draw a baby bird and an adult bird.

<table>
<tr><td>baby</td><td>adult</td></tr>
</table>

b) I can describe different ways in which vertebrates change as they grow older.

I can name four stages in a frog life cycle.

_______________________   _______________________

_______________________   _______________________

6 I understand that nutrition is a life process and that different animals have different diets.

I know this because giant pandas

eat _______________________ and lions eat

_______________________.

Plants

Plants can be very big or quite small. There is a huge variety of plants in our world. Most plants are green. Some plants have bigger leaves than others. Many plants have flowers, but some do not. Trees are plants that are tall and woody.

In this topic we will learn:

- the names of some parts of a plant
- that some plants have flowers
- that plants can grow from seeds and bulbs
- that plants need water, light and air to grow well
- that humans and animals eat plants for food.

Choose two key words from the box above.
Write or draw what they mean.

1 Draw a line and write the word to label a **leaf**, the **roots** and the **stem** of this plant.

2 a) Which part of a plant traps sunlight?

____

b) What do plants use sunlight to do?

____

3 a) Why do plants need a stem?

____

b) What does this plant have on
    its stem?

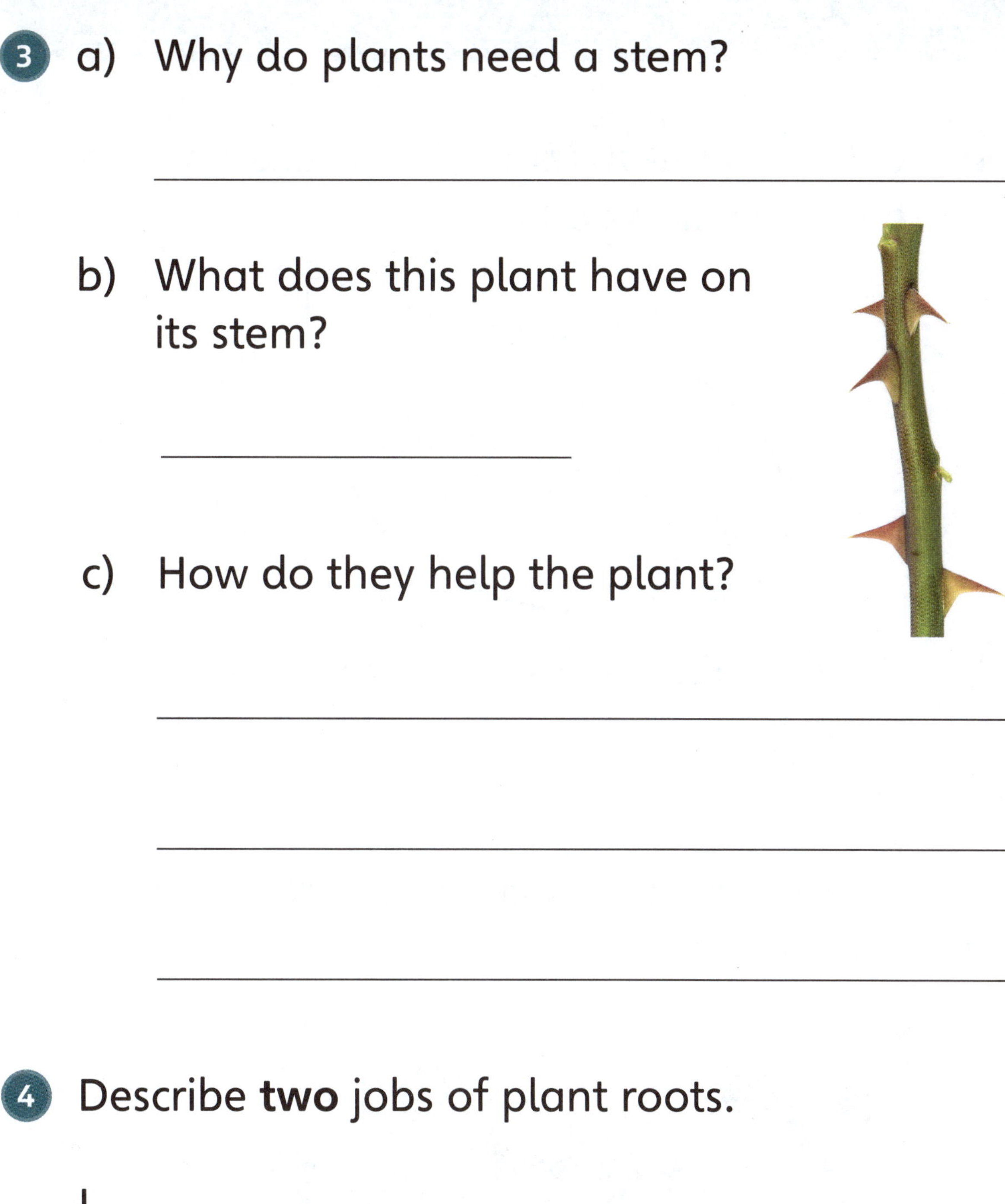

____

c) How do they help the plant?

____

____

____

4 Describe **two** jobs of plant roots.

1. ____

2. ____

Leaf shapes

1. a) Colour this leaf. Make it look like one that grows where you live.

b) Draw a label line to the largest vein.

Write vein.

2. Circle leaves that look like ones growing near your home or school.

3 Use the key to write the correct name under each leaf picture.

_________________________   _________________________

_________________________   _________________________

Flower shapes

1 Circle the picture that shows a living flower.

2 a) Draw **one** line from the word to label **one** petal.

petal

b) (i) Circle the flower most like the one in part a).

(ii) Why did you choose that flower?

____

3 Class One count flowers of different colours in a garden.

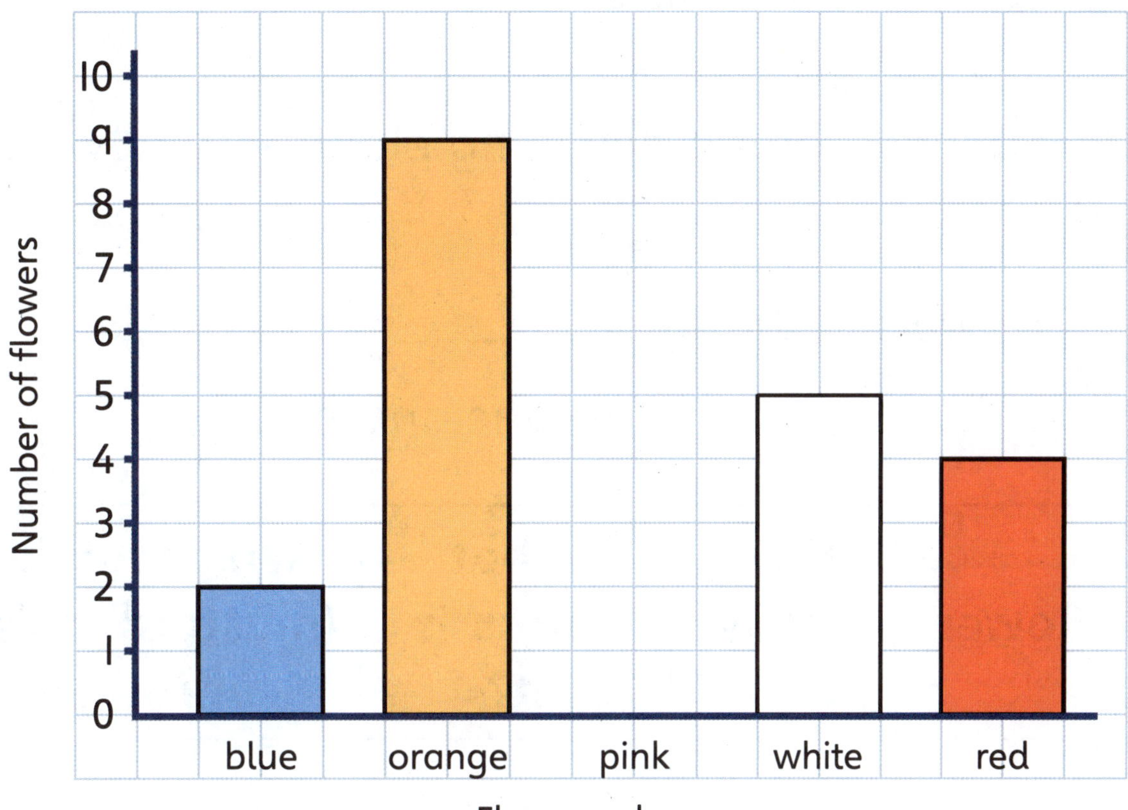

a) How many **blue** flowers did they count?

b) They counted six **pink** flowers.

Draw the bar for **pink** flowers.

c) How many flowers did they count altogether? Show the sum that you do.

Answer ________________

Flower families

1. Complete the sentences and the table.

Scientists group flowering plants into flower

___________________.

Flowers in the same ___________________ look

___________________ to one another.

Flower	How many petals?	What colour is it?	Which family (mustard, daisy or rose)?

2 Class One choose their favourite flower and record the results in a tally chart.

Flower	Number of children	Totals
	||||	
							6
		||

a) Draw the missing tally and complete the totals.

b) Circle the flower that **fewest** children chose.

c) How many children are in Class One? Show the sum that you do.

Answer _______________________

1　a)　Draw a line and write the word to label the **trunk** and a **branch** of this tree.

　　　b)　Draw some **roots** on this tree.

2　Where is the bark found on a tree?

____

3　a)　What type of tree is this?　_______________

　　　b)　Label the **trunk** and the **leaves** of this tree.

4 This tree has been cut down.

a) How wide was the tree? Use the nearest big number. _________ cm

b) Name **one** piece of measuring equipment.

____

c) What happens to the trunk of a tree when the tree grows taller?

____

d) Describe the inside of this tree.

____

____

Drawing plants

1. a) Finish drawing and colouring this flower.

   b) How many petals does this flower have?

2. a) Draw one more petal on the flower below.

   b) Colour the flower.

   c) Suggest a flower family this flower could be

   grouped in. ________________________________

3 Finish drawing this leaf.

Remember to move the page so you draw **upwards** into the curve.

4 Try drawing this leaf.

Keep your pencil on the paper for each curve.

Seeds

1. This pea seed is starting to grow.

   a) What does a baby plant have stored inside the seed?

   ____

   b) Label these **four** parts by drawing a label line from each word.

   leaf   stem

   root   seed

   c) Circle the name of the part that now traps sunlight.

   leaf   root   seed

   d) Which part holds the plant in the ground?

   ____

2 Label **one** seed in each picture.

3 Emma plants some seeds.

a) What is she doing to the seeds now?

____

b) What has she put in the pots that the seeds will grow in?

____

c) Emma has some more seeds. Why do these seeds **not** grow inside the packet?

____

____

Bulbs

1. Name the plant part shown in each picture.

____

____

____

____

2. These flowers are growing from bulbs we cannot see.

   a)   Where are the bulbs?

   ____

   b)   What does the plant store in the bulbs?

   ____

c) The flowers are growing under a tree.

Write **two** things that show there is a tree.

1. _______________________________

2. _______________________________

d) Why do these plants grow and flower when there are no leaves on the tree?

____

e) Finish the drawing of one of these flowers. Colour it and label a **leaf** and a **petal**.

Healthy plants

1. What do living plants need to grow well?

________________ and ________________ and

____

2. a) Describe what has happened to this plant.

b) Draw what you think it should look like.

3. How do leaves help plants with the life process of nutrition?

4 Plant A has a light above it.

a) Draw Plant B's light.

A   B

b) Where do plants growing outdoors get their light from?

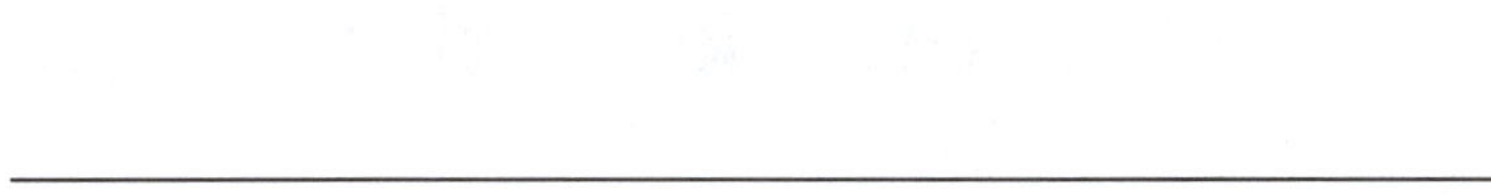

5 This plant is in water.

Describe what you can see happening.

Investigating seeds

Zola wants to investigate whether cress seeds need to be warm to grow.

First she asks a scientific question.

1 Complete the scientific question.

Do ________________ need to be ________________

to ________________?

2 a) Suggest a warm place and a cold place where Zola could put her cress seeds to grow.

warm ________________

cold ________________

b) She is changing how warm it is, so she must keep everything else the same for both dishes of seeds.

Suggest what she should keep the same.

____

____

3 Draw some cress seeds and cotton wool in the two dishes. Think how many seeds should go in each dish.

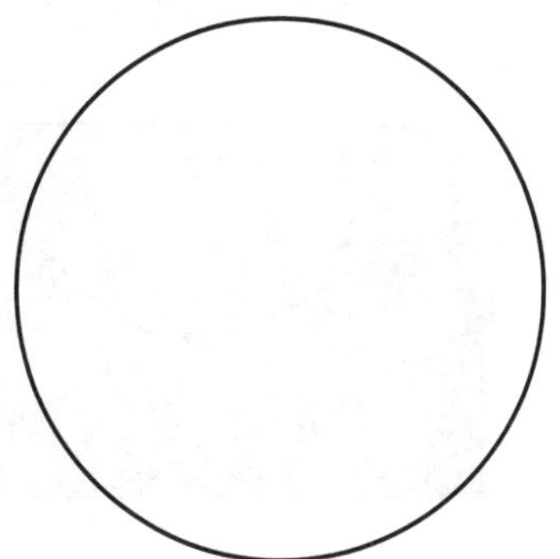

Dish A: **warm**

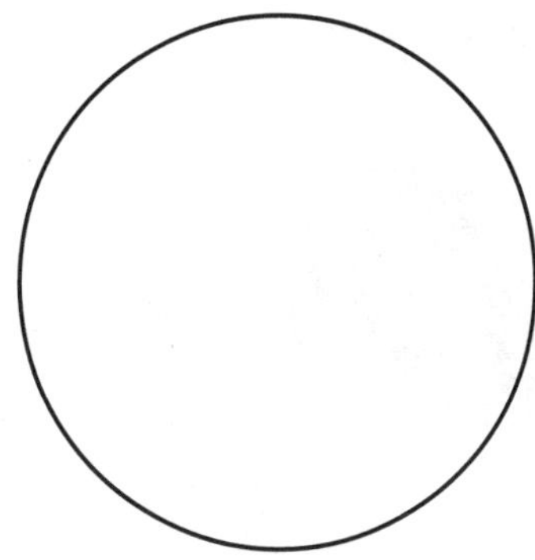

Dish B: **cold**

4 a) Should Zola put water in **both** dishes? ______

b) Give a reason. ___________________________

5 What will Zola observe and count?

____

____

6 Predict what you think will happen.

I think the seeds in Dish ___ will grow first

because _______________________________

____

Growing food

1 Draw lines to match each food with the plant it comes from.

2 a)   Where does flour come from?

____

b)   Write **two** things we can make from flour.

___________________ and ___________________

3 This is part of an olive tree.

a) Label the **branch**, a **leaf** and an **olive**.

b) Write **two** things we do with olives.

_______________________ and _______________________

4 This is part of a tree.

a) Which part of this tree
    do we eat?

____

b) Name **two** other parts of the tree you can
    see in this picture.

_______________________ and _______________________

What have I learned?

1 I know which living things are plants when I go outside or when I see pictures.

I know this because I can draw three different plants.

2 I know the names of some parts of a plant.

I know this because I can list six different plant parts.

1. _______________ 2. _______________

3. _______________ 4. _______________

5. _______________ 6. _______________

3 I understand that plants can grow from seeds and bulbs.

I know this because I can draw some seeds and a bulb.

seeds	bulb

4 I know what plants need to grow well.

I know this because I can list two things that plants need to grow well.

1. ________________   2. ________________

5 I understand that humans and animals eat plants for food.

I know this because I can list some foods from plants that I eat.

____

____

Sorting and grouping materials

The objects around us are made from materials. Objects can be made of wood, stone, plastic or glass. Our clothes are made from fabrics like wool and cotton.

In this topic we will learn:

- that objects can be made of different materials
- to name and identify some common materials
- that materials can be sorted in different ways
- that materials have different properties and how to describe them
- how to use a key to identify and group objects made of different materials.

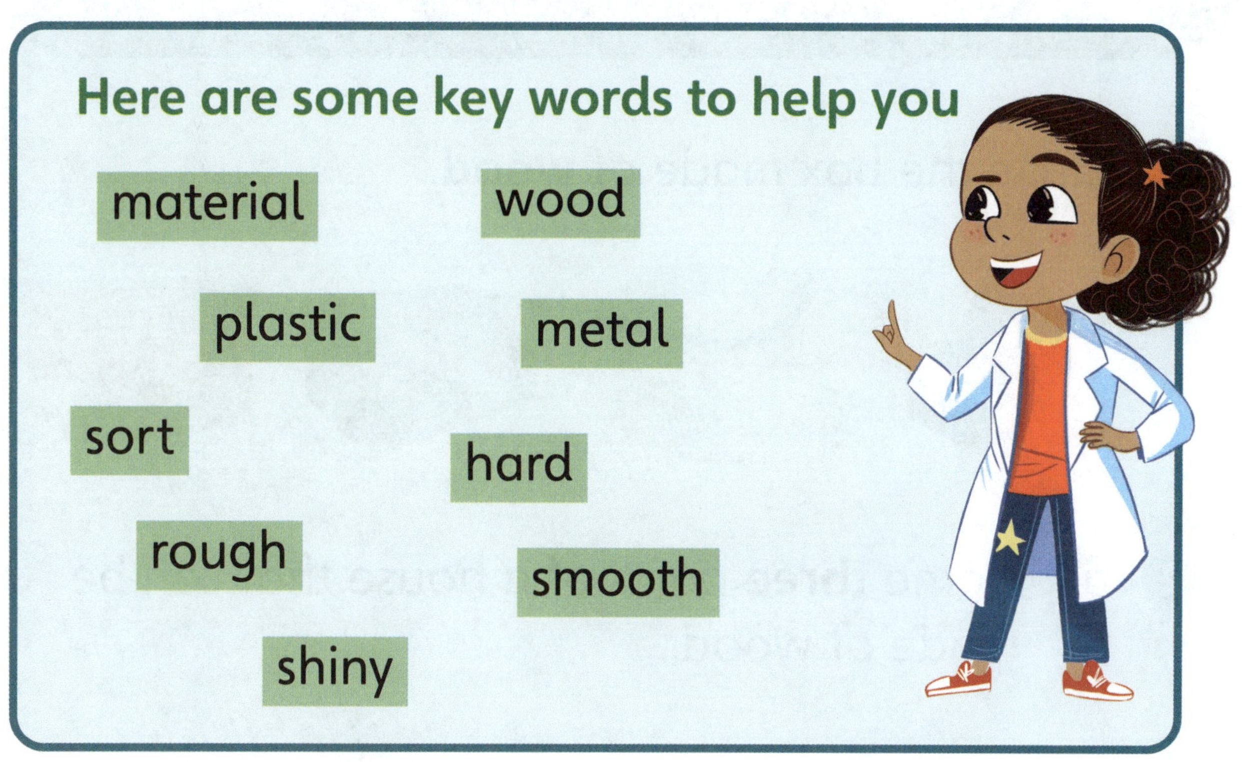

Choose two key words from the box above.
Write or draw what they mean.

Wood

1 Circle the box made of **wood**.

2 a) Name **three** parts of a house that can be made of wood.

1. _______________   2. _______________

3. _______________

b) Write **six** other things that can be made from wood.

1. _______________   2. _______________

3. _______________   4. _______________

5. _______________   6. _______________

3 Which parts of a tree does wood come from?

_______________ and _______________

4 Suggest why humans should keep planting trees.

____

____

5 Look at this pile of wood.

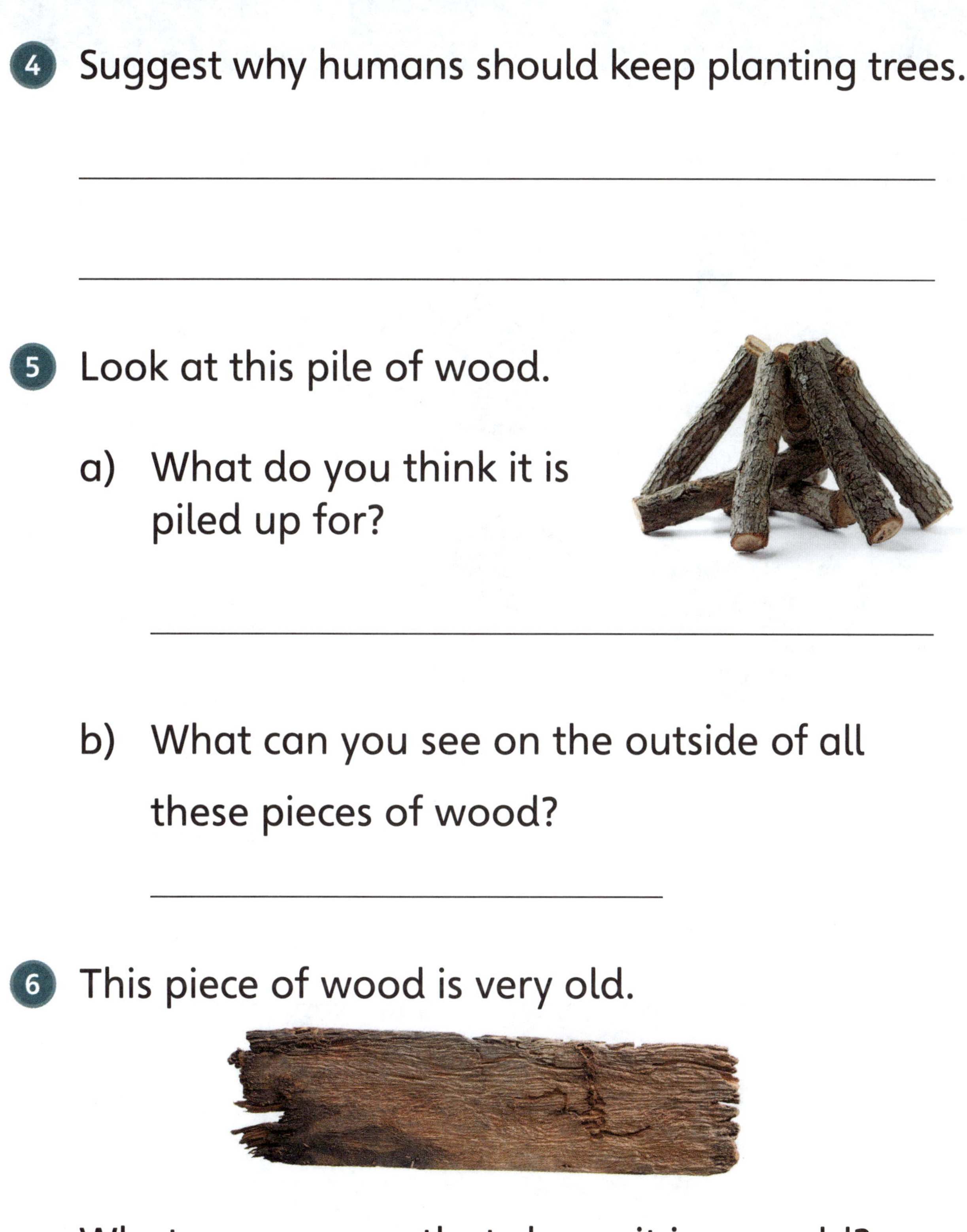

a) What do you think it is
piled up for?

____

b) What can you see on the outside of all

these pieces of wood?

____

6 This piece of wood is very old.

What can you see that shows it is very old?

____

____

Stone and glass

1 a)   Circle **two** objects made of **stone**.

b)   List **two** more things that can be made of stone.

1. ___________________   2. ___________________

2 List **four** things at home or at school that are made of **glass**.

1. ___________________   2. ___________________

3. ___________________   4. ___________________

3 a) Circle the **beaker**.

b) Who uses objects like this in their job?

____

c) What material are these objects made of?

____

4 This horse's head is made of marble.

It is very old.

a) What can you see that shows it is very old?

____

b) What type of material is marble?

____

c) Why is marble a good material to use for making this head?

____

Fabrics

1 a) Circle **one** word to describe
        this wool scarf.

        hard   cool   soft   shiny

   b) In what sort of weather do people wear a
       wool scarf?

       ____

   c) Name **two** different animals we get
       wool from.

       _______________ and _______________

2 Put one tick (✓) in each row of the table to
   show the texture of the fabrics.

Fabric	Rough	Smooth

3 a) Write **cotton** under the ball made of cotton.

b) Write **wool** under the ball made of wool.

c) Where do we get cotton from?

____

d) Name **four** things that can be made
from cotton.

1. ______________________________________

2. ______________________________________

3. ______________________________________

4. ______________________________________

Plastic

1 a) Write **plastic** above the chair made of plastic.

b) Write **wood** above the chair made of wood.

c) Write **fabric** above a chair with fabric cushions.

d) Circle the **softest** chair.

2 a) What is most plastic made from?

____

b) Describe the texture of plastic.

____

c) What colour are plastic objects?

____

3 a) Circle **two** plastic bottles.

b) Write **one** reason why plastic is **good** for making bottles and **one** reason why it is **not good**.

Plastic bottles are **good** because

____

Plastic bottles are **not good** because

____

c) Draw some other objects that are made of plastic.

Metal

1 Draw lines to match each material with something that it is used to make.

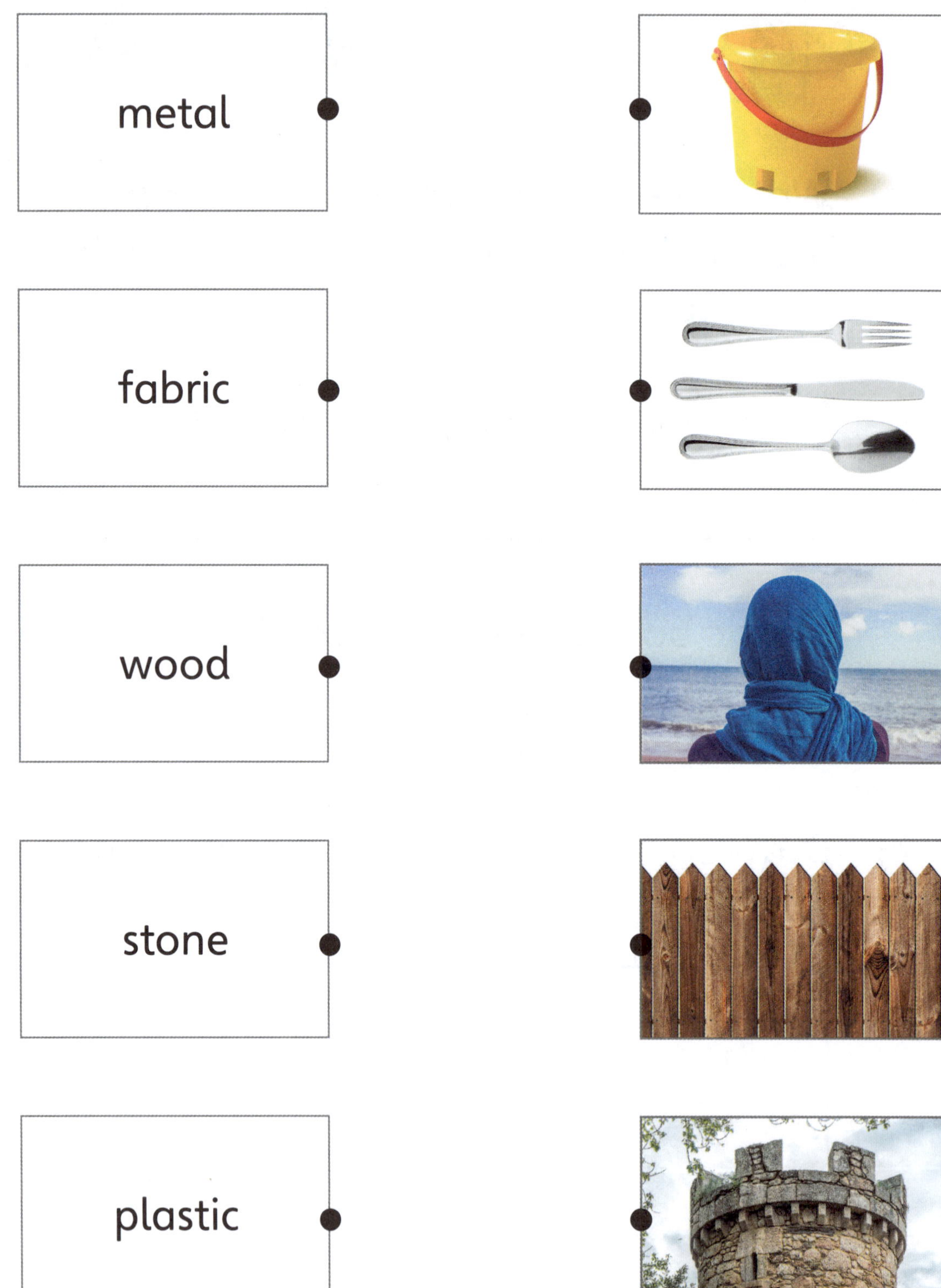

2 Circle **two** words that best describe this metal foil.

hard   rough   shiny   dull   smooth

3 Put **one** or **two** ticks (✓) **in each row** of the table to show whether the object is **rough** or **made of metal** or **both**.

Object	Rough?	Metal?

Sorting materials

1. Put **one, two** or **three** ticks (✓) **in each row** of the table to show whether the object is **soft**, **green** or **shiny**.

The first one has been done for you.

Object	Soft?	Green?	Shiny?
	✓	✓	

Use these objects again on the next page.

2 a) Draw shiny objects from the table in here.

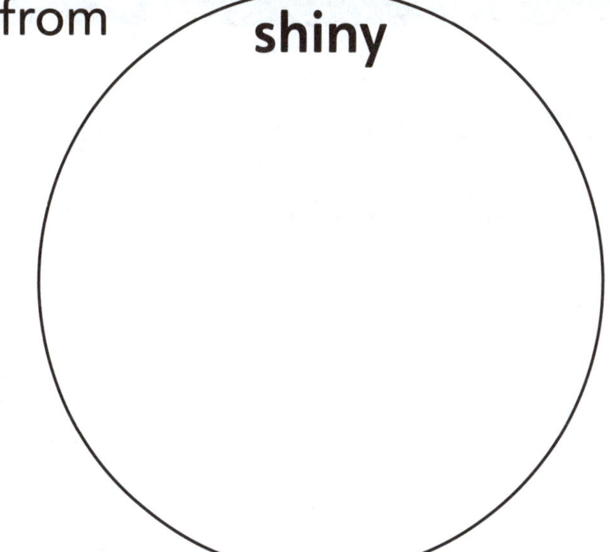

b) Draw **one** more shiny object.

3 a) Draw the soft objects and the green objects in here.

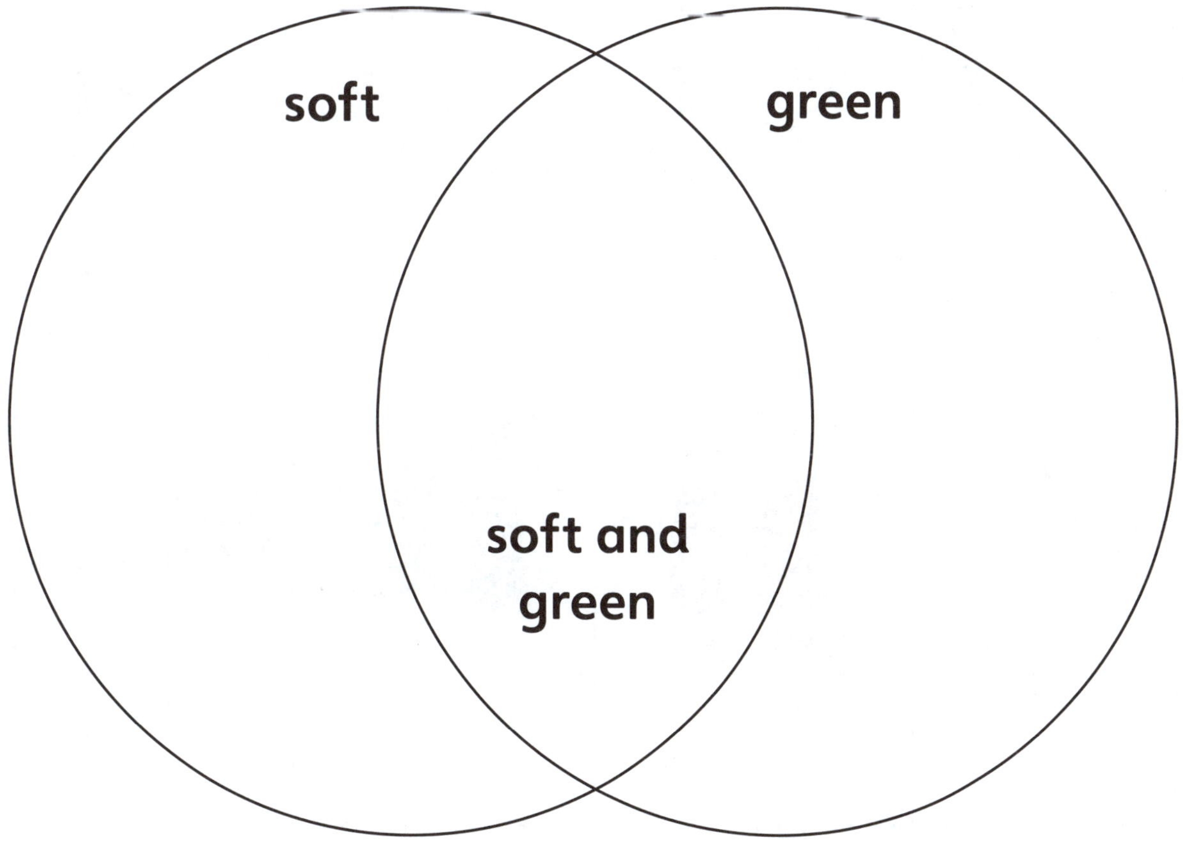

b) Draw **one** more object in each section.

Using a key for materials

1 Use the key to write the correct letter under each object.

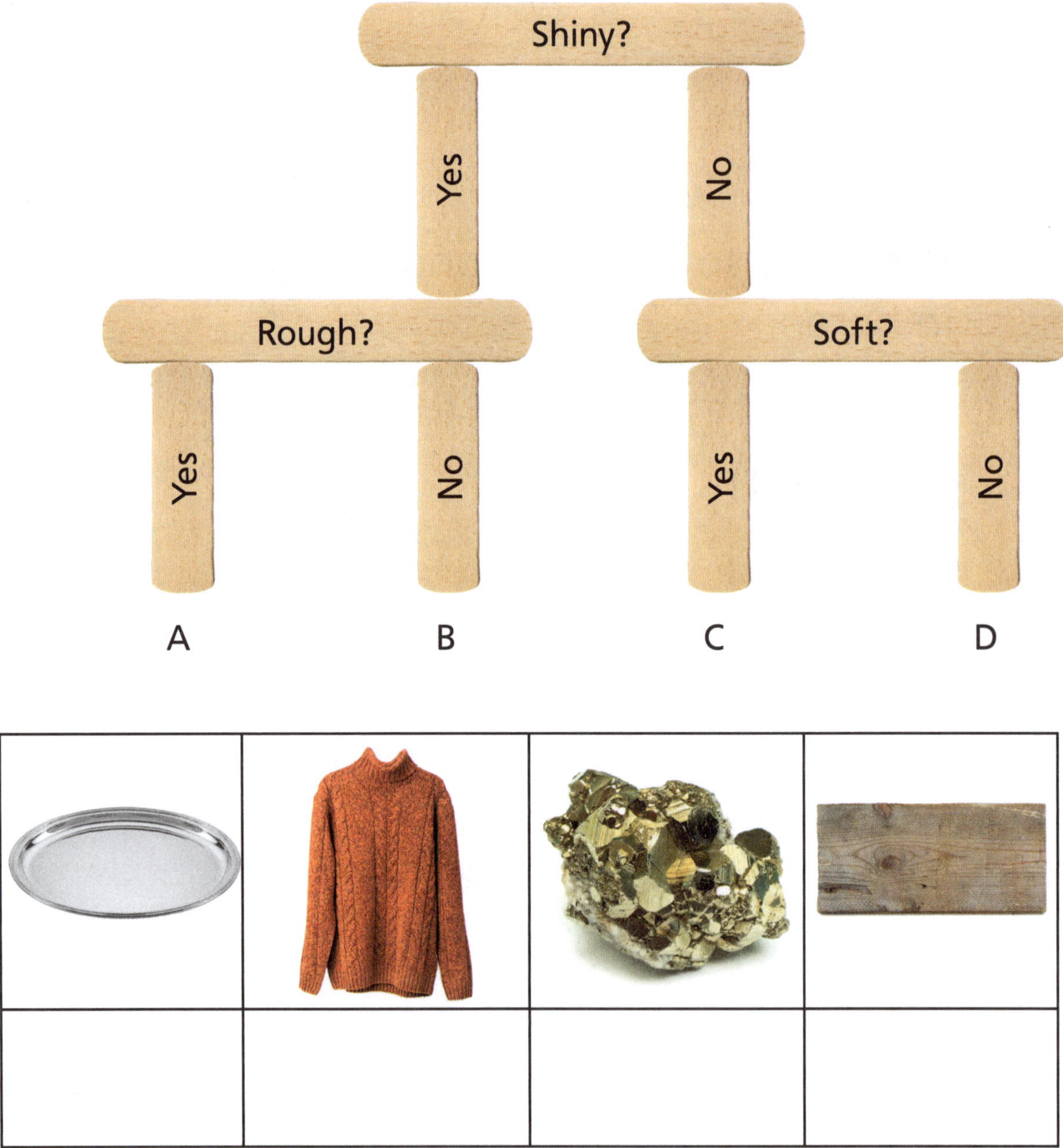

2 Use the key to write the correct letter under each object.

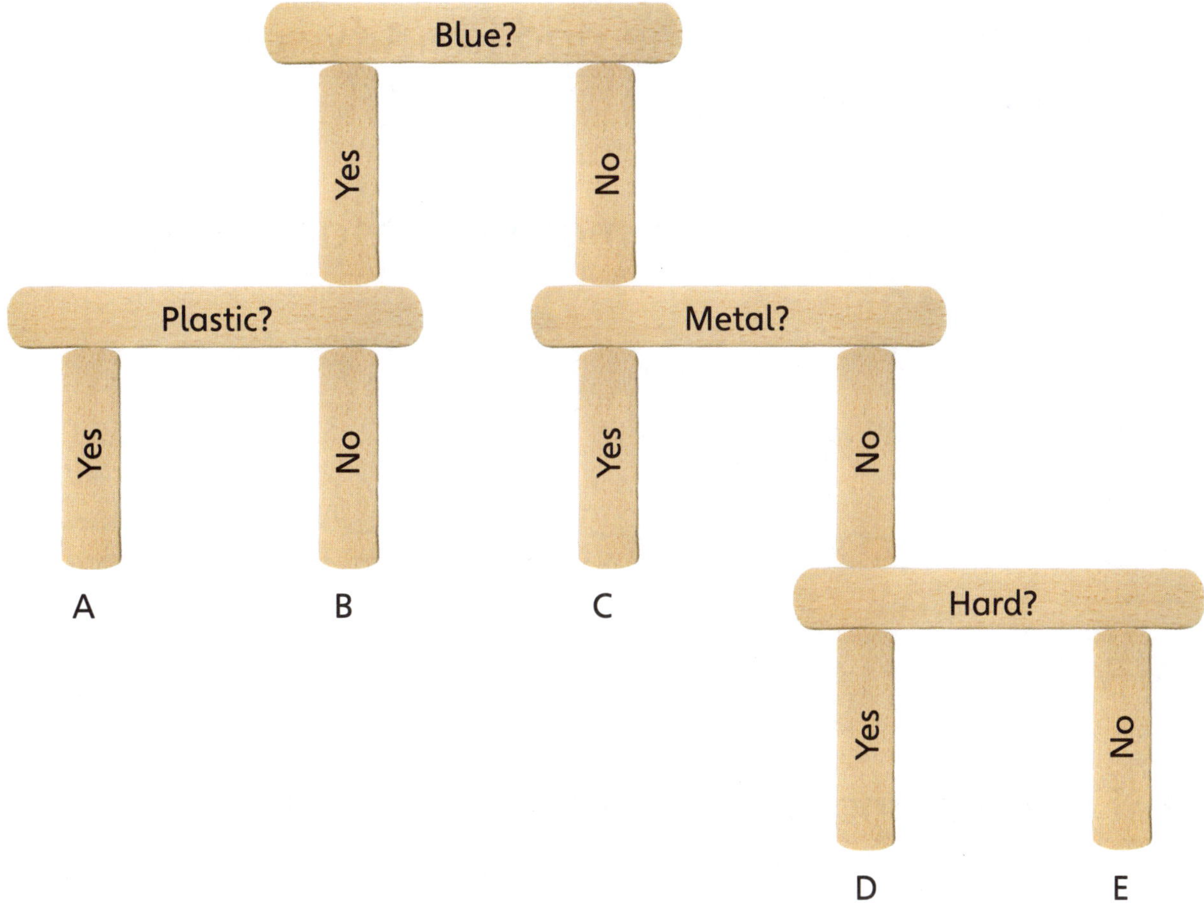

What have I learned?

1. I know that objects can be made of different materials. I can name and identify some common materials.

I can list six different materials that things can be made of.

1. _______________________   2. _______________________

3. _______________________   4. _______________________

5. _______________________   6. _______________________

2. I understand that materials have different properties, and I can describe them.

I can write one or more words to describe three materials.

material	word or words to describe it
_______________	_______________________________
_______________	_______________________________
_______________	_______________________________

3 I understand that materials can be sorted in different ways.

I know this because I can draw some objects in these circles.

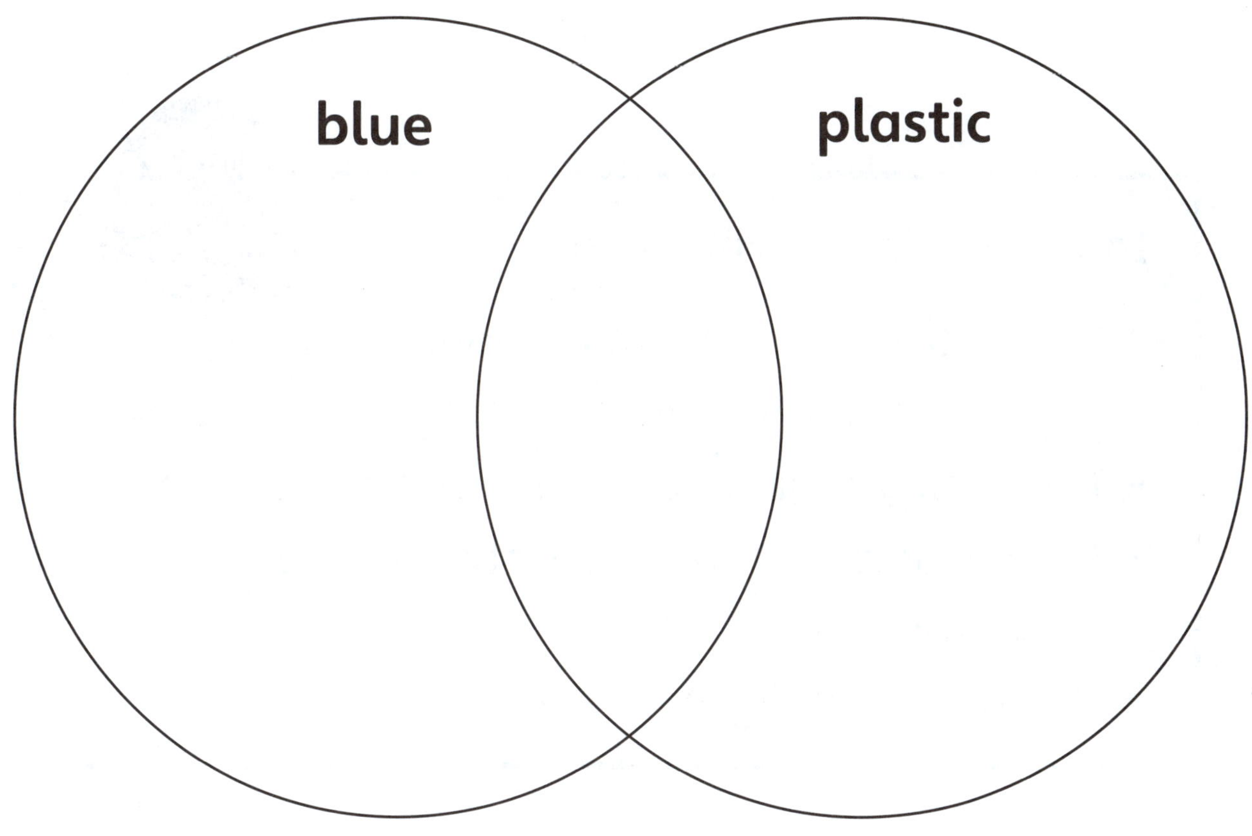

4 I can use a key to identify and group objects made of different materials.

I know this because I can answer yes or ______ to questions about the properties of different materials.

Light and dark

Light comes from a source. A light source is something that makes its own light. Light from the Sun is all around us every day, but at night it is dark.

In this topic we will learn:

- that light comes from a source
- to identify some sources of light
- that shiny objects are not sources of light
- to compare differences between night and day
- that we need light to see.

Choose two key words from the box above.
Write or draw what they mean.

Sources of light

1 a) Which sense organ detects light?

____

b) What do we need light to help us to do?

____

c) What is the scientific word for a place that light comes from?

____

d) Draw **two** different places that light comes from. Label what the places are.

2 a) A mirror is **not** a source of light. Why not?

____

____

b) Write the names of these six objects in the correct circle below.

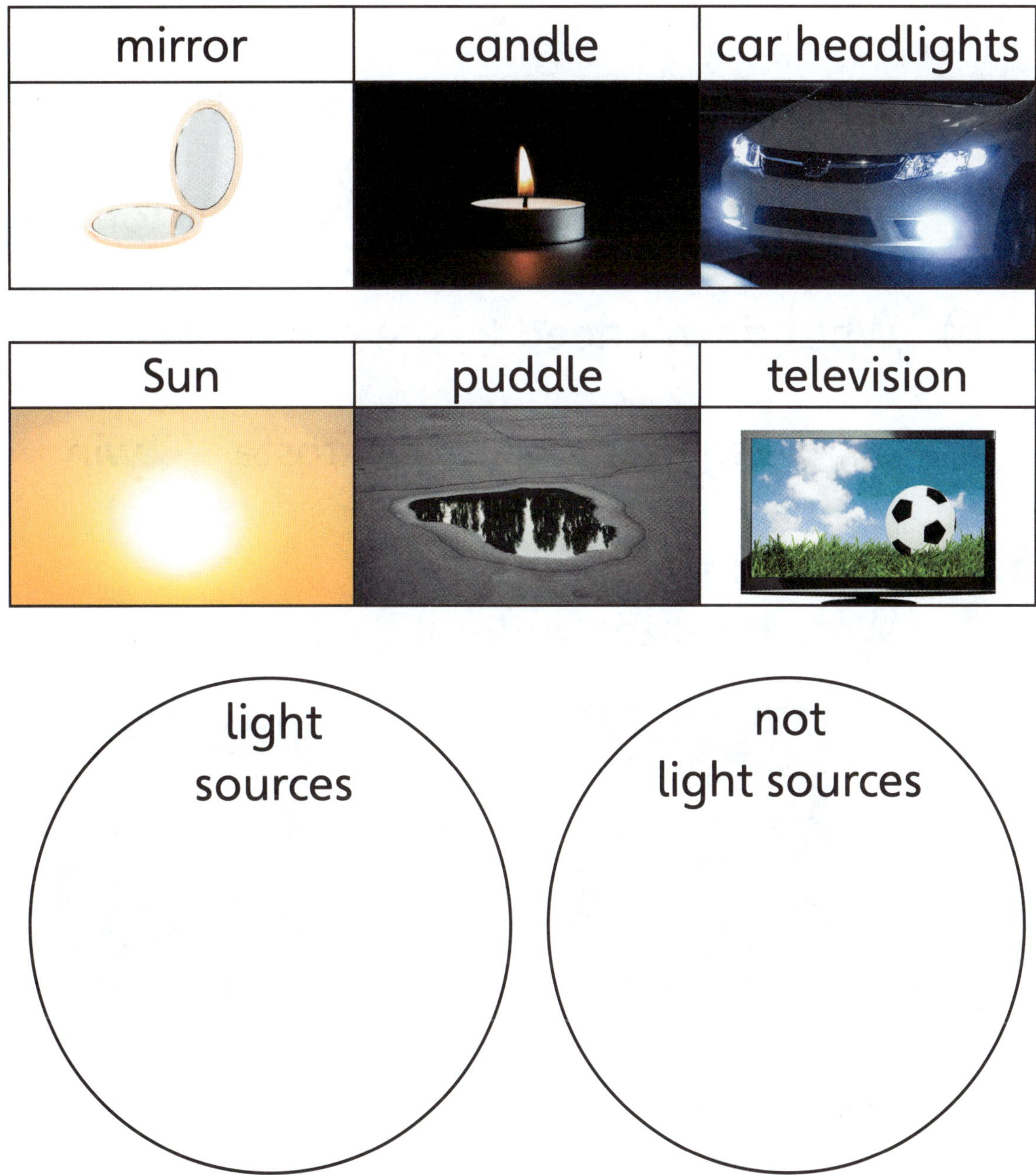

c) Why do these circles not overlap?

____

____

Bright lights and dim lights

1 Circle **one** answer each time.

   a) Which sense organ detects light?

      ears   eyes   nose   skin   tongue

   b) What do we need to see an object?

      air   light   sound   taste   wind

2 a) Which light is brighter?
Write **brighter** under it.

_______________   _______________

   b) Write a word under the other light to compare it to the brighter one.

   c) Name the glasses that some people wear in bright sunlight.

____

3 Put **one** tick (✓) in **each row** of the table to show whether the light named is **bright** or **dim**.

Light		Bright?	Dim?
floodlights			
candles			
fireworks			
street lights			
sunlight			
paper lanterns			

Shiny objects

1 Draw one line from each object to show whether it is **shiny** or a **source of light**.

shiny

source of
light

2 Write **one** word in each space.

Light can travel through ________________ and

________________.

When light bounces off an object, we say the

object ________________ light.

3 a) What does this kitten see in the mirror?

____

b) Is this mirror a source of light?

____

4 Describe what is happening in this picture.
Are there **two** candles?

____

____

____

____

Light and dark

1. Complete the sentences using some words from the box. Use a word **once** only.

> dark   ears   light   shine   see
>
> bright   hear   sound   eyes

We use our _________________ to see things.

At night it is _________________ because there is no _________________.

It is very hard to _________________ in darkness.

We need _________________ light to see well.

2. These people are walking inside a cave.

   a) Suggest why they have a torch.

   ____

   b) What will this picture look like if the torch is switched off?

   ____

3 Tick (✓) the meaning of the word *dark*.

	a place where the Sun shines
	a warm place

	a windy place
	a place with no light

4 These cars are driving through a tunnel.

Which **two** sources of light help the drivers to see?

1. _______________________________________

2. _______________________________________

5 This rabbit is outside the hole where it lives.

Compare the outside of the hole with the inside.

Outside the hole it is _______________.

Inside the hole it is _______________.

Earth and Sun

1. Circle the source of light for Earth.

2. a) What are the blue parts on this picture of Earth?

____

b) What are the white parts?

____

c) What shape is Earth?

____

d) Suggest where the camera was to take this picture.

____

3 The picture shows Earth and the Sun.

a) Label the **Sun** using a line and the word.

b) Use lines and the words to label the part of Earth that is **light** and the part that is **dark**.

c) Why should we never look directly at the Sun?

____

4 a) Describe where the Sun is in this picture.

____

b) How do you know the Sun is there?

____

Night and day

1 Part of this picture shows day and part shows night.

a) Write **day** or **night** in the spaces under the picture.

_______________________   _______________________

b) Write **two** things that show it is night.

1. _____________________   2. _____________________

c) Write **two** things that show it is day.

1. _____________________   2. _____________________

2 Class One make a model to show day and night.

torch   **globe**

a)   Complete the sentences about the model.

They use a torch to represent the ___________.

They use a globe to represent ___________.

b)   Describe what scientists mean by a *model*.

____

____

c)   Colour in the part of the globe where it is night in this model. Use a dark colour.

d)   Find out the name of a city where it is day when it is night where you are.

____

What have I learned?

1. I understand that light comes from a source.

   I know this because a light source is something that makes its ________________

   ________________.

2. I can identify some sources of light.

   I know this because I can list **four** things that are sources of light.

   1. ________________   2. ________________

   3. ________________   4. ________________

3. I know that shiny objects are **not** sources of light.

   I know this because shiny objects do not make their ________________ ________________.

   Shiny objects ________________ light.

4 I know that the Sun is the source of light for Earth.

I know this because places where the Sun is not shining are _________________.

5 I can compare differences between night and day.

I know this because I can describe night and day using these pictures for help.

Night _____________________________________

____

Day _____________________________________

____

6 I understand that we need light to see.

I know this because when there is no light it is _________________ and we cannot _________________ things.

Pushes and pulls

Humans move in many ways. We can make objects move too. We can push an object. We can pull an object. Pushes and pulls are the forces that make objects move.

In this topic we will learn:

- to describe different ways of moving
- that pushes and pulls can make objects start or stop moving
- that pushes and pulls are forces
- to identify some examples of pushes and pulls.

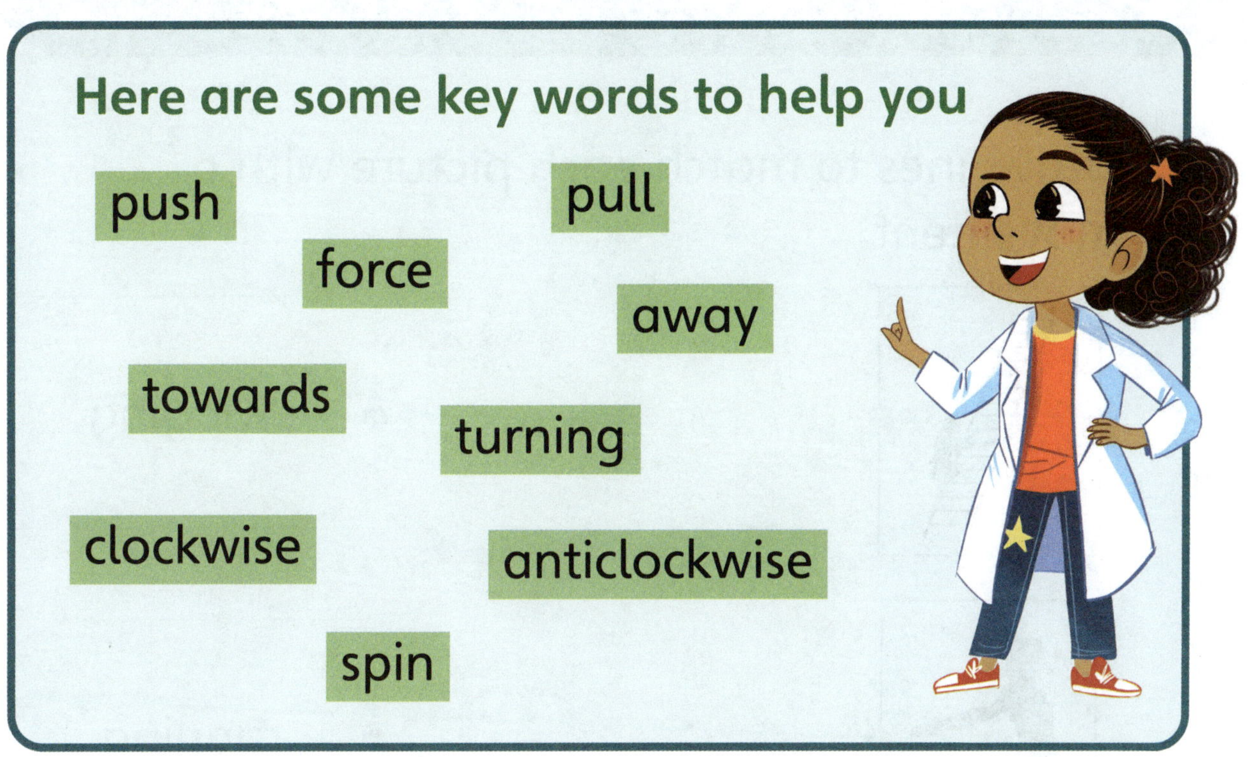

Choose two key words from the box above.
Write or draw what they mean.

Fast and slow

1 Draw lines to match each picture with a movement.

2 These animals move in three different ways.

Complete the tally chart for their movements.

Movement	Tally	Total
walking	⊬⊬ l	
flying		
jumping		

Total number of animals =

Moving toys

1. Draw an arrow to show how each toy moves.

Toy	Way it moves

2 Draw some other toys that move.

3 This playground toy has three different parts.

Draw someone moving on each part.

Starting to move

1. How can the parent start this swing moving?

____

2. What is the scientific word for pushes and pulls?

____

3. The boy and the ball are not moving.

   a) How can he make this ball move?

   ____

   b) How can he make his wheelchair move?

   ____

   c) How can someone else make his wheelchair move?

   ____

4 The ball is rolling towards some bowling pins.

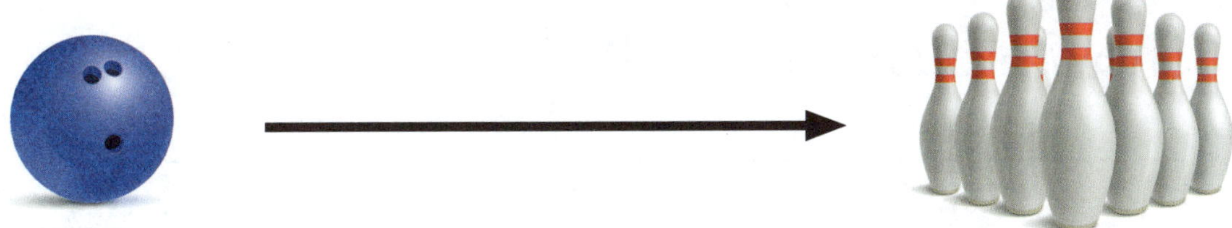

a) What happens to the bowling pins when the ball hits them?

____

b) Predict what happens if the ball is rolled with a big pushing force and with a very small pushing force.

Draw the bowling pins.

Big force	
Very small force	

Pushes and pulls

1. Put **one** tick (✓) **in each row** of the table to show a **push** or a **pull**.

Picture	Push	Pull

2 These workers are moving a box.

a) Circle the arrow showing which way the box moves.

b) Write **pushing** or **pulling** to show what each worker is doing.

A __________________   B __________________

3 a) This stone is not moving.

Explain why.

____

b) How could they make the stone move?

____

Moving in circles

1. Circle **one** toy that moves in the same way as this Ferris wheel.

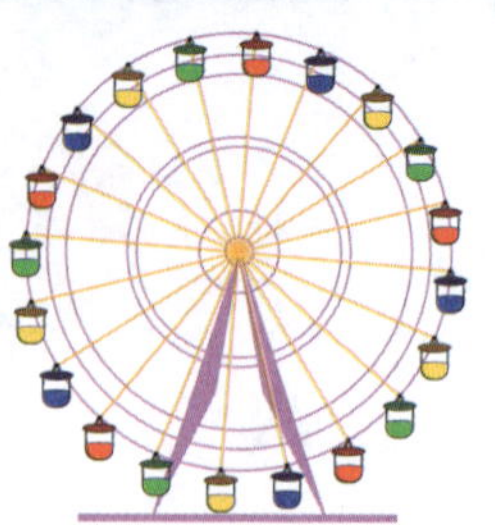

2. Mia holds the handle of this toy.

a) She moves the toy this way: ➡

Is she pushing or pulling? ___________________

Do the wheels go clockwise or anticlockwise?

____

b) She moves the toy this way: ⬅

Is she pushing or pulling? ___________________

Do the wheels go clockwise or anticlockwise?

____

3 The hamster runs inside the wheel.

a) Describe what happens to the wheel as the hamster runs. Include the direction too.

____

____

b) What happens to the wheel when the hamster runs **faster**?

____

4 This is used to choose which team starts in a game.

The spinning arrow is pointing at the blue space.

a) What colour is **one** space

   clockwise from blue? ___________________

b) What colour is **two** spaces **anticlockwise**

   from blue? ___________________

What have I learned?

1   I can observe and describe different ways of moving.

    a) I know this because I can list **four** different ways that humans move.

        1. _______________________________________

        2. _______________________________________

        3. _______________________________________

        4. _______________________________________

    b) I know this because I can draw **three** toys that move in different ways.

2 I know that pushes and pulls can make objects start or stop moving.

I know this because a football does not move

until it is _________________ or _________________.

football ——

3 I know that pushes and pulls are forces and I can identify some examples of these forces.

I know this because I can draw something being pulled and something being pushed.

pull

push

(key: b-bottom; c-centre; l-left; r-right; t-top)

Non-Prominent Image Credit(s):

123RF GB LIMITED: Avelkrieg 24 1t, 24 2t, 24 3t, 24 4t, 25 1t, 25 2t, 25 3t, 25 4t, Benjamin Simeneta 33 L T-B 4, Tadeusz Wejkszo 98 L T-B 2, Balint Roxana 34b, Fx5218 14c, Svetlanais 125 T-B 3, Jesus David Carballo Prieto / 123rf.com 11 L-R 2c, Cathy Yeulet 38t, tanyar30 117 L-R 1b, darnellvfx 11 L-R 1b, Irina Ukrainets 28 T-B 4b, 29 T-B 4t, dzein 146t, Daniil Peshkov 114 T-B 1, Alex Bramwell 49t, Yotrak Butda 104 L-R 4t, dennisjacobsen 54 L-R 2t, Nednapa Chumjumpa 130 L-R 4t, Timolina 82 L-R 3t, Allan Swart. 125 T-B 1, arkstart 104 L-R 2t, Panya Jampatong 34c, macrovector 23 L-R 4t, Bschonewille 130 L-R 2t; **AMIT JOHN:** Amit John 14t, 62b, 86b; **ARVIND SINGH NEGI/RED REEF DESIGN STUDIO:** Arvind Singh Negi/Red Reef Design Studio 22t, 47c, 66c, 23 L-R 3t, 32 L T-B 3; **Alamy Images:** Elena Kozyreva 138 T-B 1; **GETTY IMAGES INCORPORATED:** Westend61 91c, Images By Tang Ming Tung/Stone 20c, OkinawaPottery/E+ 142t, Alina Kotliar/iStock 32 L T-B 5, Natalie_/ iStock 32 L T-B 4; **MOHD SUHAIL:** Mohd Suhail 8b; **PDQ DIGITAL MEDIA SOLUTIONS LTD:** PDQ Digital Media Solutions Ltd 80t; **PEARSON EDUCATION LTD:** Sophie Bluy 40 L-R 1t; **RATAN MANI BANERJEE:** Ratan Mani Banerjee 28t; **SHERYL JOHN:** Sheryl John 12t; **SHIVANI ANSHUK:** Shivani Anshuk 32 R T-B 1; **SHUTTERSTOCK:** Annaev 92 L-R 1c, Olga_gl 13 L-R 4t, Ttstudio 5 L-R 3t, 13 L-R 1b, lyly 50 L-R b4, Le Do 92 L-R 1t, Emilio100 84 T-B 3, 85 B L-R 3, 85 T T-B 3, M88 92 L-R 2t, Vishnevskiy Vasily 60b, 61b, 54 L-R 1t, Dizzy_Studio 123 C L-R 2, Fahng_S 82 L-R 2b, Reamolko 27c, Veniamin Kraskov 106 B L-R 1, Matveev Aleksandr 113 B T-B 3, Irina Maksimova 12 L-R 2b, Africa Studio 108t, 142c, Olha Rohulya 28 T-B 1b, 29 T-B 1t, zhu difeng 87c, oksana2010 84 T-B 2, 84 T-B 4, 82 L-R 1b, 85 B L-R 2, 85 B L-R 4, 85 T T-B 2, 85 T T-B 4, Nowik Sylwia 144 T-B 3, 144 T-B 5, DenisNata 33 R T-B 4, Anna Lurye 21 T-B 1, 40 L-R 4t, Olaf Simon 84 T-B 1, 85 B L-R 1, 85 T T-B 1, Daniel Prudek 11 L-R 2b, seeyou 105t, shaineast 139t, 139t, 139t, Chz_mhOng 50 L-R b3, solarseven 126 T-B 6, Anton Starikov 126 T-B 5, Nattika 114 T-B 2, stefanphotozemun 40b, Eladora 138 T-B 5, 144 T-B 6, Rakota 139t, 139t, 139t, Roselynne 48 T-B 1, Palo_ok 98 R T-B 3, MaxVasylenko 146t, Burkina 23 L-R 2t, Sever180 110 L-R 3t, Angelo Gilardelli 117 L-R 5b, Patcharapa 104 L-R 3t, Niphon Subsri 6 L-R 1t, HappyPictures 4 L-R 3c, Miriam Doerr Martin Frommherz 10b, volkova natalia 99t, Alex Staroseltsev 106 B L-R 3, Marina Lohrbach 110 L-R 1t, Anastasiya Shubina 140 T-B 2, angelo gilardelli 116 L-R 1b, jsalasberry 147b, Valentyn Volkov 92 L-R 2c, ANURAK PONGPATIMET 12 L-R 1b, S-F 8t, 117 L-R 2b, Michael Dechev 123 T L-R 1, Jorge R. Gonzalez 129b, Xaki646 46 T-B 2, Alexandr Junek Imaging 13 L-R 1t, Red Confidential 39b, sarayut_sy 81 L-R 2c, Vadzim Mashkou 108 T-B 2b, sciencepics 78c, Oleksandr But 27t, Tenstudio 32 L T-B 5, Miceking 56 T-B 1, Teevakul T 68t, Boriss Jepifanovs 146t, Photomaster 62 L-R 2t, Kuttelvaserova Stuchelova 62 L-R 4t, Erik Lam 33 R T-B 1, Anton Vasylenko 146t, Makc 7b, 7t, Chones 109 L-R 1t, 109 L-R 3t, 91 L-R 2t, Iurii Kazakov 59b, Kalos2 6 L-R 3t, Sunflowerr 143t, 143t, xpixel 51 L-R b3, Ihor Hvozdetskyi 12 L-R 2b, Nataly Studio 98 L T-B 4, Neshcheret Mariia 91b, ZILEAN 95b, Xseon 59t, Ewa Studio/ Shutterstcok 127t, Hintau Aliaksei 126 T-B 2, Dimijana 11 L-R 1c, Nagel Photography 13 L-R 2t, Kovaleva_Ka 98 R T-B 4, Marius Steinke 123 C L-R 1, Martin D Brown 92b, Italika 140 T-B 1, anat chant 48 T-B 4, Net Vector 15b, ducu59us 144 T-B 7, aarrows 146t, 138 T-B 2, AlenKadr 111 L-R 1t, nbiebach 63c, Kazoka 48 T-B 5, weter 777 58 1t, Eric Isselee 12 L-R 2b, Loskutnikov 6 L-R 2t, Julio Aldana 4 L-R 2c, Koverninska Olga 72t, Juris Kraulis 60t, 126 T-B 3, Sdecoret 131t, Rajesh Narayanan 111 L-R 3t, sergograph 125 T-B 2, humbak 94t, Vitalii Hulai 33 R T-B 3, Ivan Kurmyshov 123 T L-R 3, 64t, 46 T-B 1, 46 T-B 3, 46 T-B 4, 13 L-R 2b, 50 L-R b2, 58 L T-B 2, 58 R T-B 3, Scisetti Alfio 82 L-R 3b, 98 L T-B 3, BlueRingMedia 47b, 65t, Josh McCann 11 L-R 1t, Natan86 106 B L-R 2, Gunnar Pippel 51 L-R b1, Milart 9 T-B 1, Sawitree Promphithukkul 9 T-B 4, KKulikov 58 L T-B 1, 58 R T-B 2, sevasaves1 48 T-B 2, Robert Eastman 4 L-R 3t, 33 L T-B 3, 58 L T-B 3, Yuriy2012 138 T-B 3, YURI HRIDNE 133 L-R 1t, Bonita R. Cheshier 129t, Real Vector 112 T-B 1, Kazakova Maryia 12c, 12c, 12c, Birgit Reitz-Hofmann 8 L-R 2c, SCOTTCHAN 104 L-R 1t, Vadarshop 146t, Videowokart 82c, Akila_Yan 6 L-R 4t, Tsekhmister 48 T-B 3, 52, soul_studio 111 L-R 4t, Stocksnapper 98 R T-B 1, Michal Sanca 138 T-B 4, matka_Wariatka 46 T-B 5, Sebastian Studio 30 T-B 4b, Cherstva 144 T-B 1, 144 T-B 4, Kruglov_Orda 51 L-R b4, Maja H.. 82 L-R 2t, Tankist276 54 L-R 2c, 8 L-R 4c, JGA 112 T-B 5, Hit003 124 L-R 1c, 124 L-R 2c, Ugorenkov Aleksandr 117 L-R 3b, Heavypong 145t, Mountain Brothers 141B, Iness_la_luz 99b, Seroff 82 L-R 4b, Macronatura.es 11 L-R 2c, Julia Sanders 56 T-B 2, Apple2499 8 L-R 3c, Ala Sharahlazava 56 T-B 3, La corneja artesana 90c, Danny Smythe 114 T-B 5, Tartila 135 L-R 1c, 135 L-R 2c, Bogoshipda 109 L-R 2t, Pandapaw 50 L-R b1, 108 T-B 1b, Mogens Trolle 72c, Roman Samokhin 30 T-B 2b, AlexAvich 116 L-R 2b, Picsfive 109 L-R 4t, hugo_34 81 L-R 1b, Vitaliy Snitovets 9 T-B 2, Duntrune Studios 123 T L-R 2, Peter Hermes Furian 27t, nexus 7 123 C L-R 3, beton studio 4 L-R 1b, Chokniti-Studio 54 L-R 1c, wavebreakmedia 21 T-B 2, 40 L-R 2t, Elena Zajchikova 132c, Hanapon1002 5c, 21 T-B 3, Lipsett Photography Group 4 L-R 2b, arka38 106 T L-R 2, NisanatStudio 28 T-B 2b, 29 T-B 2t, Steve Collender 140 T-B 4, Yesaulov Vadym 4 L-R 5c, Chansom Pantip 81 L-R 2b, Eric Isselle 33 L T-B 2, Pixelspieler 106 T L-R 1, Alex prokopenko 8 L-R 1c, IrinaK 4 L-R 1c, 58 R T-B 1, Kamira 107c, ideyweb 140 T-B 5, S_Photo 30 T-B 5b, Koshevnyk 56b, Burana Srivakul 4 L-R 2t, vovan 125 T-B 5, Tony Campbell 12 L-R 2b, Motacat 39t, Pedal to the Stock 113 B T-B 2, Tsekhmister 4 L-R 3b, 4 L-R 4c, 62 L-R 1t, Christos Georghiou 56 T-B 4, evkaz 106 T L-R 3, Skylines 113 B T-B 1, Toey Toey 22b, Andrew Burgess 33 L T-B 5, Hissiyat Gezgini 127b, irin-k 33 L T-B 1, fuyu liu 125 T-B 4, photo25th 110 L-R 2t, Ociacia 10t, My Life Graphic 105b, Janis Smits 15t, RoleArt 33 R T-B 2, OljaS 79t, Volga 98 L T-B 1, Linda Bucklin 11 L-R 2t, Quang Ho 82 L-R 4t, Barry Barnes 144 T-B 2, gresei 149t, Mikhail Mishchenko 140 T-B 6, Sonate 116 L-R 4b, Ching Design47 32 L T-B 2, Martina_L 9 T-B 3, Lolostock 112 T-B 3, Bannykh Alexey Vladimirovich 140 T-B 3, Milan noga 130 L-R 1t, Dirk M. de Boer 13 L-R 3t, Sergiy Kuzmin 113t, laschi 139t, 139t, 139t, Patrick Kirby 125 T-B 6, Shuttertum 107t, donatas1205 111 L-R 2t, Sergey Melnikov 32 L T-B 1, illustrissima 23b, me-1 110 L-R 4t, vitaliy_73 114 T-B 4, Ivonne Wierink 62 L-R 3t, 2xSamara.com 146t, Petr Malyshev 82 L-R 1t, NIK 51 L-R b2, chatgunner 131b, Lifestyle Travel Photo 126 T-B 1, LUIS PADILLA-Fotografia 11 L-R 1c, Kanea 80b, Sunny_baby 114 T-B 3, Vaclav Matous 5 L-R 1t, Sergey Skleznev 117 L-R 4b, foxaon1987 130 L-R 3t, Gala_Kan 30 T-B 1b, Denis Radovanovic 116 L-R 3b, Sergej Razvodovskij 112 T-B 4, Patpitchaya 9 T-B 5, Mariait 5 L-R 2t, grey_and 112 T-B 2, Lukasz Szwaj 98 R T-B 2, Karkhut 128b, Oleksandr Lytvynenko 4 L-R 4b, Annet_ka 95t; **STEPHEN WONG:** Stephen Wong 30 T-B 3b; **TSZ-SHAN KWOK:** Tsz-shan Kwok 133 L-R 1t; Tsz-shan Kwok 133 L-R 2t; **UTSAV ACADEMY AND ART STUDIO:** Utsav Academy and Art Studio 86t

All other images © Pearson Education.